ANTIBLACK RACISM AND THE AIDS EPIDEMIC

Antiblack Racism and the AIDS Epidemic

State Intimacies

Adam M. Geary

First published in 2014 by
PALGRAVE MACMILLAN®
in the United States—a division of St. Martin's Press LLC,
175 Fifth Avenue, New York, NY 10010.

Where this book is distributed in the UK, Europe and the rest of the world,
this is by Palgrave Macmillan, a division of Macmillan Publishers Limited,
registered in England, company number 785998, of Houndmills,
Basingstoke, Hampshire RG21 6XS.

Palgrave Macmillan is the global academic imprint of the above companies
and has companies and representatives throughout the world.

Palgrave® and Macmillan® are registered trademarks in the United States,
the United Kingdom, Europe and other countries.

ISBN: 978–1–137–38952–7

Library of Congress Cataloging-in-Publication Data is available from the
Library of Congress.

A catalogue record of the book is available from the British Library.

Design by Newgen Knowledge Works (P) Ltd., Chennai, India.

First edition: May 2014

10 9 8 7 6 5 4 3 2 1

for Steve

Contents

Acknowledgments

The genesis of this book has been much longer than its size would suggest, and along the way I have benefitted from kindnesses that I am happy to acknowledge.

The problem I pursue here emerged from critical questions raised but not answered in my dissertation in the History of Consciousness at the University of California at Santa Cruz, directed by Teresa de Lauretis and with Donna J. Haraway and Gary Lease as supportive committee members. I appreciate their patience, persistence, and encouragement.

At the University of Arizona, my primary intellectual community has been the Subjectivities, Sexualities, and Political Cultures faculty research cluster sponsored by the UA Institute for Lesbian, Gay, Bisexual, and Transgender Studies. Over the years, this research cluster included Bram Acosta, Maribel Alvarez, Laura Briggs, Caryl Flinn, Anne-Marie Fortier, Carlos Gallego, Laura Gutiérrez, Miranda Joseph, Liz Kennedy, Adela Licona, Eithne Luibhéid, Sallie Marston, Araceli Masterson, Spike Peterson, Hai Ren, and Sandy Soto—an extraordinary group of people to learn with.

Writing is lonely; writing groups help. At the point that I gave up revising my dissertation, I was involved in a writing group with Jennifer Roth-Gordon, Susan Shaw, Victor Braithberg, and Marcela Vasquez. As I struggled to complete what emerged, I was writing with Miranda Joseph and Susan Stryker. I hope that I was as helpful to them as they were to me, and I appreciate all of their generosity and good humor.

The writing of the book also benefitted from support from the College of Social and Behavioral Sciences at the University of Arizona, in the form of a Junior Faculty Development Leave, and from the UA Department of Gender and Women's Studies, in the form of the Mary Bernard Aguirre Professorship made possible through the generosity of Rowene Aguirre-Medina and Roy Medina.

Friendships have sustained me. Elizabeth Castelli ushered me into my future; after these many years, I try to honor her friendship, generosity, and kindness by paying it forward. In Tucson, I have been lucky to be surrounded by wonderful people, including Michelle Berry, Anne Stolcis, Alison Futrell, Andy Wedel, Adam Ussishkin, Gus Tzamouranis, Chris Rush, Victor Lodato, and Eleni Hasaki. I also want to thank the staffs of the local coffee houses: Raging Sage, Sparkroot, Caffe Luce, and Exo Coffee Roasters. Nicole Guidotti-Hernández has been my coconspirator and dining companion. The long phone calls and extended visits with Karen Kim have made life more wonderful through our many years of friendship. Jared Sexton is a treasure, kind and brilliant.

My mother, Ilene Geary, has always been a source of support and encouragement. I thank her for cheering me on as I advanced through academic training, employment, and accomplishments. My father, Jed Geary, has always been there when it counts.

My life is infinitely richer and happier for the daily presence of Steve Johnstone in it. He makes me laugh a lot! This book is dedicated to him.

Chapter 1

Rethinking AIDS in Black America

The color of AIDS in America is black. Of the approximately 1.2 million people in the United States currently living with the Human Immunodeficiency Virus (HIV), nearly half (46%) are black as are nearly half of all people newly infected with HIV each year, even though African Americans account for only 12 percent of the total US population.[1] As with the global pandemic,[2] there are more black people living with HIV in the United States than whites or any other racial-ethnic group. The prevalence rate for African Americans is nearly eight times greater than for whites and three times higher than for Latinos.[3] Broken down by gender, the numbers are even more extreme. Nearly 75 percent of those in the United States living with HIV are male. Prevalence rates for black men are dramatically higher than for any other group of people: six times the rate for white men and three times the rate for Latino men. Black women suffer an HIV prevalence rate only exceeded by black men. Black women's prevalence rates are 18 times greater than those of white women and four times those experienced by Latino women.[4] Black women's prevalence rates are nearly 50 percent greater than Latino men's, the next highest group.

Rates of new infection (incidence rates) closely parallel prevalence rates. Black people suffer about 45 percent of all new HIV infections, while whites account for 35 percent and Latinos 20 percent. New infection rates are greatest for black men, whose rate of infection is six and a half times higher than for white men and more than two and a half times that of Latino men. As with prevalence rates, the incidence rate for black women is dramatically disproportionate to all other women. Black women are infected with HIV at rates more than 15 times higher than white women, and nearly three and a half times higher than Latino women. At current rates, one in 16 black men and one in 32 black women are likely to be diagnosed with HIV in their lifetimes.

What theory of disease epidemic can help us understand the racial blackness of the US AIDS epidemic? Or, more pointedly, how does the racial blackness of the US epidemic challenge what we think we know about it? How do these numbers challenge what we mean when we say "AIDS"?

In what follows I argue that the racial blackness of the US AIDS epidemic has been produced not by the behaviors of African Americans but by conditions of structured, racist domination. Racism, not race, ethnicity, or culture.[5] In dominant social and scientific discourses, HIV infection has been understood to index perverse intimacies of sex and drug use, what are politely named "risk behaviors." AIDS has been considered a consequence of these intimacies. For black Americans, however, I argue that the primary structuring factor that has determined risk of HIV infection has been what I call *state intimacy*, or the violent intimacy of the racist state. From structured impoverishment to racial segregation, and from mass incarceration to the "political death" meted out to former prisoners, the state has structured the ways in which black Americans have been made vulnerable to HIV exposure and infection far beyond the capacity of any individual or community mitigation or control. This structured vulnerability entirely exceeds questions of so-called risk behaviors or their social construction.

The AIDS epidemic is structured not by the *deviant* behaviors or relations that people engage in, but by the *unequal and violent conditions* in which they are forced to live and that are embodied as ill-health and vulnerability to disease. Medical anthropologist and physician Paul Farmer has described HIV disparities as the biological expression of social inequalities, a position that resonates strongly with the nation's racial demographics of suffering.[6] While this is an essential starting point for any critical account of AIDS or other disease phenomena, to say that the racial distribution of the US AIDS epidemic indexes social inequality is simply to begin a discussion. That black people suffer disproportionately is not accidental or an intensification of otherwise "colorblind" forces of social inequality; it is a direct consequence of the centrality of antiblack racism in structuring the conditions of possibility and the conditions of continuance for this epidemic, conditions with social and health consequences for everyone, but especially for black people. This is not a conspiracy theory: I do not mean that AIDS is a plot to eliminate black people. What I mean is that antiblack racial formation—the organization of relations of violence, domination, and exploitation directed at people who are marked "black"[7]—has structured the conditions of living and dying that have enabled this epidemic, conditions that cultural theorist Lauren Berlant has recently named "slow death."[8] Although not exclusively a consequence of antiblack racism, antiblack racism has nonetheless been fundamental in structuring the conditions of possibility for the nation's epidemic.

How to Have Black Materialism in an Epidemic[9]

A sustained account of AIDS for black Americans transforms what we know the AIDS epidemic to be, how it travels, and who it affects. Medical historian Elizabeth Fee and epidemiologist Nancy Krieger have described the dominant way of thinking about and responding to HIV risk as betraying a "biomedical individualism."[10] As Krieger describes it, the biomedical model has three key features:

> It emphasizes biological determinants of disease amenable to intervention through the health care system, considers social determinants of disease to be at best secondary (if not irrelevant), and views populations simply as the sum of individuals and population patterns of disease as simply reflective of individual cases. In this view, disease in populations is reduced to a question of disease in individuals, which in turn is reduced to a question of biological malfunctioning. This biologic substrate, divorced from its social context, thus becomes the optimal locale for interventions, which chiefly are medical in nature.[11]

HIV risk discourses have been thoroughly biomedical. They tend to individualize risk by treating it as the consequence of personal behaviors. They exhibit an isolated understanding of viruses, as though they were more or less self-contained biological machines that operated the same way under any and all conditions. And they tend toward an isolated understanding of human individuals in their interactions with viruses, as though the conditions of their meeting was irrelevant.[12] Both the actions of people and the actions of viruses are stripped of context, focusing attention on the nature of the virus and on the acts that potentially allow transmission of HIV from person to person. Group patterns, in turn, appear "simply as the sum of individual traits and choices."[13] The key disciplines for thinking about and attempting to intervene into the risk of HIV have been virology, psychology, and ethnography. Given the ongoing failure to create a vaccine for HIV, in turn, the primary method of intervening into the epidemic has been targeted, therapeutic modification of acts and the reformation (or punishment) of those members of society who engage in them: all those strategies that have gone under the name of "AIDS prevention."

In the biomedical common sense of HIV risk, the disease disparities experienced by black Americans can only be understood as an index of their so-called risk behaviors. Medical anthropologist and physician Didier Fassin, describing this common sense as applied to Africans, might just as well be speaking of African Americans, when he writes,

> *Ordinary culturalism,* on the one hand, explained the epidemic in terms of cultural specificities supposedly shared by all Africans or, sometimes, limited within ethnic boundaries. *Commonsense behaviourism,* on the other hand, restricted its focus to attitudes and practices disconnected from social realities. Both neglected the historical dimensions of the disease, its socio-economic determinants, its political implications.[14]

Black Americans too have suffered under the neglect of ordinary culturalism and commonsense behaviorism. Even if never stated explicitly, cultural and behavioral pathology have been presumed to be the cause of black HIV rates, as they are of other forms of black suffering. Always, the presumption is that black people experience higher rates of HIV because of what they do (or do not do), how often they do it (or not), and with whom. But black people's experience of vulnerability to HIV is irreducible to numbers of HIV-transmitting acts, numbers of sexual partners, or numbers of concurrent sexual relations. It must be understood within the social determinants of health. Black people individually and collectively suffer kinds of increased malnutrition, concurrent infection, and overall immiseration that lend toward increased susceptibility to HIV infection.[15] This health inequality is recognized as contributing to disease progression (black people progress from initial infection to advanced HIV disease faster than nonblacks), quality of care (black people are less likely to receive advanced care than nonblacks), and death rates (black people die earlier than nonblacks),[16] but racially unequal health and healthcare must also be recognized as significantly structuring risk and vulnerability to infection as well. Poorer health, in fact, would account for the repeated inability in epidemiological studies to establish behavioral differences between black and nonblack populations in the United States that would account for racialized HIV disparities. Instead of behavioral difference, HIV disparities emerge from the structuring of ill health for blacks and the manner in which ill health increases vulnerability to HIV infection. Thus, critical analysis and political intervention must shift from attention to the structuring of risk behaviors and to the material structuring of health as the key condition for the HIV epidemic in the United States, as it is globally.

The understanding of black illness and disease as resulting from racist social relations has a long history. In his sweeping history of black urban health, medical historian David McBride traces a continuous black health tradition from the late nineteenth century to the present.[17] While this tradition has evolved over time, from its earliest articulation it argued against racialist theories that reduced black ill health or disease to either black biological difference (so-called race) from nonblacks or black cultural pathology (so-called culture or ethnicity). Rather, black ill health and disease patterns were understood as emerging from racist inequality and domination. As W. E. B. Du Bois wrote at the turn of the twentieth century, "The Negro death rate and sickness are largely matters of condition and not due to racial traits and tendencies."[18]

As McBride's history demonstrates, the black health tradition has been one of the primary—if not the singular—vehicles for a materialist analysis of health and disease in the United States. The materialist tradition in health science "define[s] the *social causes and origins* of health and disease, relating them to the power relations in society."[19] For instance, Frederick Engels, in his masterful study of the conditions of life for the mid-nineteenth-century working classes of Manchester, England, presented a detailed analysis of the etiology and epidemiology of typhoid, tuberculosis, scrofula, and rickets as "part of an overall analysis of the working and living conditions of the working class under capitalism. He specifically related disease to the social relations of production and class structure they determined. Since the problem resided in capitalism, real solution required transcending capitalism."[20] Drawing from but also extending the work of these founding authors, materialist health science has challenged and continues to challenge medicalized understandings of health and illness that treat disease as biological events that obey natural laws (positivism in the health sciences), insisting on their social structuring. Disease and epidemic are "social events" and entirely dependent on the social production of necessary conditions.[21] They cannot be reduced to an agent (like a virus) and its "natural, biological, and harmonious laws,"[22] let alone to kinds of people and their natural or unnatural dispositions.

Although the terms "materialist epidemiology" or "materialist health science" are rarely used anymore, even by those within the tradition that relates itself to the founding work of Du Bois or Engels, I want to reclaim those terms.[23] More commonly, health studies that insist on the social origins of disease and health are produced under different names: the social determinants of health and disease; the political economy of health; social medicine; and social epidemiology.[24] These other terms, while indexing real distinctions in theoretical and practical orientation, also index a more or less explicit distancing from the Marxist, materialist tradition. At times, the difference appears to be mostly strategic, carrying out materialist analysis but under another name, one that might, for instance, be funded by the bourgeois institutions that control health knowledge and health research in the United States and globally. More often, though, materialist analyses that take place under these other names pacify the social conflict determining the conditions that they study as foundational to health and disease. Those conditions of health and disease are reduced to a listing of proximal causes without an overall structure or engine; or, in the words of epidemiologist Nancy Krieger, a "web of causation" without a "spider."[25] While this research may assist in understanding

micro-level conditions that structure health and disease susceptibility, it fundamentally obfuscates the structured social relations
through which those conditions are produced, often leading to
medical interventions into the effects of social inequality while
functionally protecting that inequality.

A materialist epidemiology of the AIDS epidemic, and especially
of racialized disease disparities, departs completely from biomedical epidemiology, with its narrow, fetishistic focus on virus and
behaviors. Whereas materialism situates health and illness within
contexts formed from social inequality and argues for intervening
in those contexts to improve health or fight disease, biomedicine
tends to scale in toward isolated biological entities when examining disease and health, from the isolated human individual to
the isolated virus, bacterium, or other disease agent. Biomedicine
"de-socializes" health and illness, treating viral disease epidemics
as simply the transmission of virus from individual to individual
on a mass scale. Both virus and individual body are abstracted
as points on a grid that are connected through transmission vec-
tors. The contact chart is a favorite visual technology. What comes
into focus in biomedicine, then, are the nature of the viral agent
(treated as an "object" in the positivist sense) and the mechanism
of transmission, treating infection (successful transmission) as a
calculable effect of exposure. The two hands of biomedicine, in
turn, are behavioral interventions into transmission mechanisms
and high-tech, pharmaceutical attacks on viruses and other disease
agents. What biomedicine leaves out is the biosocial context in
which human bodies become vulnerable to disease agents, including viruses, if exposed to them.

Materialist epidemiology places the presence of disease in persons or groups within a social context, understanding disease
incidence (e.g., HIV infection rates) as more than a simple representation of *exposure* to an infectious agent. Rather, infection
patterns depend on the general health of populations of people
prior to exposure, in addition to the specifics of the disease agent.
(In virology and epidemiology, this is referred to as "agent factors" and "host factors.") Individuals and groups of people are
exposed to disease agents relatively randomly and relatively often,
but those agents generally only emerge as diseases, let alone epidemics, in welcoming sociobiological conditions, especially the

welcoming condition of human bodies made vulnerable through malnutrition, environmental poisoning, parisitosis, and other indices of impoverishment and social violence. Any given individual's susceptibility to an infectious agent will depend in part on the mode of exposure and the qualities of that agent, but also on her or his general health and ability to ward off infection prior to exposure, as well as the general health of others nearby. The great advances in population health, especially in the twentieth century, were predicated on raising the general health of populations through social investments in drinking water, nutrition, safe housing, sanitation, and environmental safety, among other social investments. Population health, not the behaviors of individuals or small groups, is widely understood to be a primary determinant in transformations in the history of diseases in human beings. While other forms of immune compromise may increase disease susceptibility for an individual, epidemics generally require kinds of population-level vulnerability that come from political, economic, and environmental immisseration.

This is as true of the AIDS epidemic as it has been for other disease epidemics. Compromised health better explains the extremely disproportionate HIV rates for black people in the United States, independent of behaviors. Compromised health has been shown to increase the likelihood that exposure to HIV will result in infection and to increase an individual's infectiousness to others, if living with HIV. Over the long term, compromised health within a given population will lead to greater disease burden in it, even if this population engages in the same distribution of potential transmission behaviors as healthier populations.

All of this seems to have been broadly forgotten in the AIDS epidemic, including within investigations of the overrepresentation of black people. Why? McBride argues that the failure to bring the black health tradition to bear upon the AIDS epidemic resulted from the convergence of three historical facts.[26] First, by the early 1980s, the black health tradition, and with it the broader materialist tradition in the US health sciences, had been effectively marginalized and isolated within the US health sciences.[27] This represents both the ideological hegemony of biomedicine within the US medical establishment, but also the effective isolation of the black tradition from investigations of the differentiated health of the nation.[28] To the degree that black health disparities were conceived as a problem at all, rather than simply ignored, they were treated as either the consequence of black cultural pathology or black racial-genetic vulnerability. Second, a rigorous black critique of the AIDS epidemic was blocked by the blatant racism of dominant representations of AIDS, especially the "black Haitian or African origin" theory.[29] Against the racist "blame game" directed at black people on a global scale, black communities and especially black health professionals attempted to distance themselves from AIDS altogether. Third, and finally, AIDS emerged within the most marginalized black people, those for whom the black middle class, including black medical professionals, already felt ill-at-ease: black gay men and other men who have sex with men, drug users, and the urban hyper-poor, especially poor, unmarried women.[30] What black political scientist Cathy Cohen has called "secondary marginalization," the hierarchical division within black communities,[31] meshed with the black middle class's defensive reaction to the racist representations of the purported origins of AIDS—and therefore the blame for it—to block the black materialist analysis in favor of the easier scapegoating of so-called black deviance.

While McBride treats this as a kind of perfect storm—the unfortunate alignment of somewhat discrete historical conditions—I want to suggest that these three historical conditions formed an ideological unit that are ultimately inseparable.[32] McBride's description of the relationship between knowledge production and cultural scapegoating parallels a discursive analysis advanced by queer cultural theorist Cindy Patton to describe how knowledge about HIV risk has been contained within a discourse on "queerness," or deviance.[33] As I will describe in more detail momentarily, Patton has long tracked the ideological importance of a discourse on deviance in structuring the ways that HIV risk is described in both lay and scientific knowledge. Revelation of HIV infection, individually and collectively, is always treated as a revelation of deviance, especially sexual deviance but also drug use. Patton argues that this "queer paradigm" has functioned ideologically to restrict investigation of the social structuring of the risk of HIV infection and interventions into that structuring of risk. The cultural work of queerness has, therefore, been to support a particular way of knowing disease risk: the biomedical way. The stereotyping of deviance so widely evident and so regularly bemoaned in AIDS risk studies and AIDS cultural politics is no error. It is a necessary discursive prop for a way of knowing risk centered upon what people do—to borrow from the French theorist Michel de Certeau, their "practices of everyday life"[34]—rather than upon the material structuring of life worlds through relations of inequality, exploitation, and structured violence—their *conditions of everyday life*.[35] This suggests that the pathologization of black deviance was not simply contemporary to the marginalization of the black health tradition in the earliest years of the AIDS epidemic; pathologization was and continues to be an ideological necessity for blocking that materialist tradition and supporting a biomedical interpretation that focuses on kinds of people (so-called risk groups) and the deviant things that they do (so-called risk behaviors). The story of black deviance precluded a materialist analysis of vulnerability to disease as structured by antiblack racism.

The biomedical scapegoating of deviance cannot simply be set aside at this point, however, as nearly all of the knowledge that we have about the AIDS epidemic has been shaped by it. Biomedical knowledge production has been entirely dominant in the history of the US epidemic, as with the global one, and has structured the way that AIDS is represented as a problem for analysis and intervention, or *government* in the Foucauldian sense.[36] This is especially true of incidence and prevalence data collected and organized by a presumed transmission category, which is to say more or less all official data collected by state and international organizations. This data abstracts scenes of exposure to HIV from their biological and social context, reifying the act that might expose one to HIV as itself inherently risky. What is lost is the context: not just the structuring context of those acts but the enabling biological context that allows a virus to successfully infect human bodies that, if well and healthy, exhibit significant immunological resistance to it. What we are left with, then, is evidence without context, or without the right kind of context. Where biomedical individualism situates behaviors within individual psyches or coherent cultures ("of deviance" is never said but always presumed), a materialist critique attempts to recontextualize transmission within a material context of how certain people are made vulnerable to infection, which in turn is irreducible to exposure. Getting to the materialist account of the racial structuring of the AIDS epidemic, then, demands that we work through and beyond the queer paradigm, undoing a form of representation that has not only structured most of the knowledge that has been produced about the epidemic but also an affective form that has supported that knowledge.

Beyond the Queer Paradigm

A series of stereotypes have appeared with some regularity to "explain" the severity of the AIDS epidemic in black America:[37] the whispers of "rough" sex (said to be "like Africans," but unlike white Americans or Europeans);[38] the secretly bisexual man on the "down low"; the compensatory, hypermasculinity of urban black men;[39] the black women disempowered in the marriage market by high rates of male incarceration, vulnerable to eligible black men's caprice;[40] or the superabundance of inner-city drug use and risky sex.[41] But to understand the role of these stereotypes we need look no further than the current information page on the AIDS epidemic among African Americans hosted by the US Centers for Disease Control and Prevention (CDC), which engages the same cultural logic if in polite, sanitized form.[42]

The CDC's public, wed-based information about AIDS represents the official story that dominant society tells itself about the nation's epidemic.[43] In addition to links to statistical and demographic information, as well as basic information on HIV, social campaigns, and testing, the site addresses two kinds of subjects of HIV risk: behavioral subjects (e.g., "Gay, bisexual, and other men who have sex with men") and subjects with recognized social identities, especially racial-ethnic identities. African Americans, Latinos, and Native Americans have their own webpages and demographic information, as do Women and Transgender people. But the distinction between behavioral subjects and social identities is not clear-cut. The inclusion of "other men who have sex with men" with gay and bisexual men continues the longstanding conflation of risk behavior with social identity, as does the shift from "Injection drug use" on the main "Topics" page to material addressed to "injection drug users" and their "sexual partners."[44] Both sex between men and injection drug use are insistently contained within social identities. But if practices are consistently confused with identities, the same is also true in reverse, if less obviously. Racial, ethnic, and other social identities are also fundamentally behavioral identities. This is never said, but is the paradigmatic logic that allows all of these categories to exist together in the same discursive space and seem to make sense.

The material presented in the CDC's information on "HIV among African Americans" demonstrates the discursive slippage between racially disproportionate disease suffering and racialist understandings of behavioral difference.[45] The page begins by stating that "African Americans are the racial/ethnic group most affected by HIV," and after a brief introduction, a series of dire numbers are listed demonstrating that black men suffer the highest rates of disease prevalence and new infection in the United States; that black men who have sex with men (MSM) represent the overwhelming majority of black men newly infected with HIV and a plurality of all newly infected MSM in the 13–24 age group; that black women's new infection rates were 20 times that of white women and five times that of Latino women; and that nearly all new infections with HIV among black women were through heterosexual sexual activity. Notably, no immediate explanations are offered for these numbers, suggesting that a common sense already exists to interpret them. As I see it, this common sense makes its appearance in the order and organization of the information. It is the common sense of sexual transmission. The coupling of raced gender with sexual transmission knowledge for both black men and women signals for the reader that transmission and prevalence rates are connected to sexual activity. Thus, immediately after the dire numbers on black men's HIV burden come numbers on sexual activity between men, and immediately after the equally dire numbers on black women's HIV burden is the corresponding sexual answer: heterosexual sex, presumably with black men. Metonymy does its work, allowing proximity to function as argument. A link between disease burden and sexual activity is never argued; it is the common sense of the epidemiological evidence as it is organized and presented. It is also, of course, the basic proposition of the assertion that HIV is a behaviorally transmitted virus, and especially that it is sexually transmitted.

This biomedical, behavioral common-sense is confirmed at the end of the document as the CDC writers turn to the pragmatics of intervention. After important caveats about the role of higher prevalence rates on new infection rates and of the limiting effects of poverty on access to forms of care, including treatment for other sexually transmitted diseases, the CDC identifies "stigma" as one of the key "prevention challenges" for African Americans:

> **Stigma, fear, discrimination, homophobia, and negative perceptions about HIV testing** can also place too many African Americans at higher risk. Many at risk for infection fear stigma more than infection and may choose instead to hide their high-risk behavior rather than seek counseling and testing. (emphasis in original)

This is simply blaming the victim. African Americans are represented as illiberally intolerant, producing a climate of shame and stigma in which "high-risk behaviors" are unchecked rather than brought under the rational administration of "counseling and testing." As demonstrated carefully in Cathy Cohen's masterful study of the social divisions within black community both represented in and amplified by the AIDS epidemic, stigma is quite real and quite damaging within black social worlds, as it is beyond them. But in order for this to be a meaningful piece of information for greater disease burden in African Americans, the cultural stigmas would have to be dramatically different and more intense than in white, Latino, Asian, or Native communities, an assertion for which the CDC provides no evidence, and for which there is no evidence. It is simply a cultural stereotype about African Americans: that they are more homophobic and AIDS-phobic than nonblacks, and especially than whites. For the CDC, one of the key sexual stereotypes about blacks that explains disparate disease burden is the cultural pathology of extreme stigma and homophobia, a cultural pathology that allows and encourages "high-risk behaviors" to proliferate unchecked.

Tellingly, while "stigma" is the last of five "prevention challenges" facing African Americans, it is the dominant factor in "what [the] CDC is doing" to overcome those challenges. Other than low rates of HIV testing (for which stigma has been offered as an explanation), none of the other prevention challenges are represented in what the CDC seems to understand as its role: nothing about treatment for other sexually transmitted diseases that "significantly increase the chance of getting or transmitting HIV" or about poverty and "the socioeconomic issues associated with poverty—including limited access to high-quality health care, [and] housing." Rather, "what [the] CDC is doing" is more of the same: five of the seven key points focus on programming and resources for HIV testing and three of the seven focus on targeted prevention outreach, which is explicitly "to address stigma and raises [sic] awareness." (The first key point contains both testing and prevention outreach.) More awareness, more testing, and less stigma: these are the tasks that the CDC has set for itself, even as other factors that might determine HIV disparities slip into the account of black vulnerability as if unconsciously—the racial segregation that structures the fact that "African Americans tend to have sex with partners of the same race/ethnicity"; the lack of access to basic healthcare and treatment for other diseases, like other sexually transmitted infections (STIs), that "significantly increase the chance of getting or transmitting HIV"; the extreme poverty and lack of access to decent housing that compromise health; and overall social precarity.

The inability to conceive risk reduction in terms of interventions into poverty, racial segregation, access to basic and preventive healthcare, or safe housing—all of which are listed as "contributing to the higher rates of HIV infection"—suggests that for the CDC, as with the dominant understandings of AIDS generally, African Americans can only be conceived as a cultural group with behavioral characteristics that lend themselves to increased risks for HIV. Even if never stated explicitly, cultural pathology is presumed to be the cause of black HIV rates, as it is of other forms of black suffering. Always, the presumption, even if not stated explicitly, is that African Americans experience higher rates of HIV because of what they do and how often they do it. While the CDC's materials are studiously polite in their multicultural tolerance, even they cannot depart completely from racial stereotyping, and they lay the ground for future racist stereotypes to emerge as needed to "explain" disease disparity. Critical race scholars describe this process as the *culturalization of race*, or the way that biologized understandings of race have been transformed into cultural understandings, often with little difference in the construction of stereotypes.[46] Rather than asserting biological inferiority and superiority, this new form of racism describes the effects of racist violence and social structuring as cultural inferiority or superiority. As we see in the CDC's representation of HIV risks, and as has been the case in the long history of derogatory stereotypes about African Americans in the AIDS epidemic, racial disparities in health and disease are now described as cultural differences between blacks and whites rather than as markers of biological superiority (whites) or inferiority (blacks). Both explanations mask the health effects of white supremacy and antiblack racism by treating those health effects as essential to whites and blacks but in slightly different idioms: the former in the idiom of biology, and the latter in the idiom of culture. This is not social advancement, but simply a transformation in racist reasoning.

The culturalization of race in AIDS discourse is part of a broader logic of HIV risk that Cindy Patton has named "the queer paradigm."[47] Writing in 1985, a few years before the reclamation of the term "queer" as oppositional sexual theory and politics, Patton argued that constructions of risk in AIDS science and public discourse treats risk and infection with HIV as indices of nonnormative or queer sexuality. Generalizing the initial descriptive conflation of the emerging epidemic with gay men, dominant scientific and public discourses on HIV risk have described those found to be suffering AIDS (even before the discovery of the viral agent) as queers engaged in perverse pleasures, especially perverse sex and drug use.

The initial reporting in 1981 of a cluster of strange pneumonia cases in the CDC's *Morbidity and Mortality Weekly Report* set the stage for a particular narrative of AIDS that continues to structure dominant discourses and health policy around HIV risk. *Pneumocystis carinii* pneumonia (PCP), the pneumonia of the infamous 1981 report, is generally only found in people who have an immune system that is suppressed for some reason; as with other opportunistic diseases associated with advanced HIV disease (AIDS), it is usually unable to establish itself in a body with a healthy immune system. Indeed, its rarity, especially in apparently otherwise seemingly healthy thirtysomethings, was one of the reasons it appeared as sufficiently abnormal to warrant reporting to the CDC in that fateful June report.[48] The five pneumonia patients, two of whom had died, were immediately identified as "young men, all active homosexuals," and the authors speculated that "[t]he fact that these patients were all homosexuals suggests an association between some aspect of a homosexual lifestyle or disease acquired through sexual contact and *Pneumocystis* pneumonia in this population."[49] The authors could hardly have known how powerful, and powerfully damaging, this initial association would be. As the contours of an epidemic began to emerge within the national surveillance system, the association between the "homosexual lifestyle" and the underlying immune suppression necessary for PCP and other, otherwise-rare opportunistic diseases would be solidified by its initial name: "Gay Related Immune Deficiency Syndrome," or GRIDS. Although GRIDS would soon give way to AIDS (Acquired Immunodeficiency Syndrome), the association between AIDS and homosexuality would continue to structure both public and scientific understandings of the epidemic, if not absolutely then as one among other forms of *queerness* that would describe those who suffer and "explain" their infection.

With increasing specificity and a nomenclature elaborate enough to rival the spectacular taxonomies of nineteenth-century sexology described with relish and a touch of sarcasm by the French philosopher Michel Foucault in his *History of Sexuality*, biomedical epidemiologists have named, and thus contained, the ever-expanding set of subjects infected with HIV.[50] From the infamous 4 H's—homosexuals, heroin addicts, hemophiliacs, and Haitians—the categories continued to proliferate to "partners" of drug users, men who have sex with men (MSM), men who have sex with men and women (MSMW), black men on the "down low," women who sell sex for drugs or money (sometimes known as "prostitutes"), African polygamists, Third World women, and whatever other Other could be invented to make sure that AIDS could be blamed on its victims and their perverse behaviors.

Patton's critique is not what would become the prominent intervention of the AIDS cultural criticism of the 1990s: the (ultimately futile) attempt to distinguish risk behaviors from specific identities (e.g., distinguishing anal intercourse as a risk behavior from male homosexuality as an identity). Rather, the critical purchase of Patton's analysis has been to mark the way that identities have been mobilized in political and scientific accounts of AIDS in order to keep the concept of risk contained and marginalized

within kinds of people and their behaviors, so that the full burden for the technologies necessary to reduce risk (safe sex, latex
barriers, clean needles) might be contained within those communities suffering the epidemic, as their "responsibility" to a
"general public" at risk, not from a virus, but from these queer
Others: dangerous bearers of disease. State and global epidemiology routinely appear to distinguish transmission behaviors from
forms of identity, but for the purposes of intervening or modify-
ing those behaviors, they are always conceived as being attached
to kinds of people who engage in them. In this way, the problem
of governing AIDS was constructed as a problem of properly governing these groups who engage in behaviors. Indeed, as Patton
demonstrates devastatingly in her book *Fatal Advice*, the queer
paradigm has served on the one hand to justify restrictions on sex
education to "normal" American youths, who in their normal-
ity have been constructed as needing to be protected more from
the queering influence of sex and drug-use education than from
HIV; and on the other hand, to marginalize and "balkanize" the
identitarian, self-help strategies forged in urban gay communities
to resist and survive the epidemic.[51] The identitarian and culture-
building strategies that gay men and lesbians cultivated to respond
to AIDS, in turn,—no matter how necessary they may have been
or seemed—fit neatly into the phobic governance of the queer
paradigm and seemed to confirm it. This phobic governance was
extended in what Patton calls the "national AIDS pedagogy" to
youth of color, sex workers, and other pathologized groups, who,
rather than being protected from the queerness of risk-reduction
knowledges, were to be made, but also held, "personally responsible" for the risks they posed to others. The normal functioning of US society, and in particular, the normal functioning of
the processes of social inequality that produced "risk groups" as
groups in the first instance was to be protected at all costs.[52]

Rather than distinguishing behaviors from identities, then, I
understand Patton to be marking the ways that dominant, biomedical risk discourses corral "risk" within discursively defined
groups rather than attending to the ways that risk and vulnerability
to HIV are structured through social life and social inequality, so
that the machinery of social difference-as-inequality may be main-
tained. The structured racisms that have made African Americans

and US Latinos more vulnerable to HIV infection become, in official and public accounts, racial-ethnic pathology, in much the same way that homophobia and transphobic oppression were turned into descriptions of gay and transcultural pathologies. Analyzing what people do (incidence and prevalence statistics organized by transmission category) was and continues to be a way of *not* talking about or investigating the conditions under which people live and are made vulnerable to disease. It protects social inequality by blaming the victim. Thus, dominant risk discourses are not wrong *simply* because they misdescribe behaviors as identities or treat identities as the primary conduits to those behaviors, but also because they ideologically mask the structural forces that organize risk and vulnerability irrespective of behaviors. As long as the concept of risk is contained within the discourse of queers, there need be no investigation into the structured relations of inequality and vulnerability, like racism, poverty, sexism, and state violence, that organize and distribute social risks, including the risk of HIV infection.

The discourse on deviance and queers has fundamentally structured thinking and research on HIV risk and blocked—or attempted to block—investigations into the structuring of vulnerability. "Queerness," thus, appears much like Foucault taught us to think about sexuality: as a dense network of discourses and technologies of power through which individuals come to experience themselves and through which populations are cultivated. The queer paradigm is a "deployment" or "apparatus" for constituting subjects and populations, those both to be invested with life and care and those to be killed or allowed to die.[53] It is also, I insist—and more fundamentally for the argument of this book—an ideology in the classic sense: a distraction or covering-over of relations of domination and how they are survived, or not. Again and again, critical scholars of AIDS are forced to prove the inadequacy of sexual deviance, including the perverse pleasures of drug use,[54] for thinking the AIDS pandemic: sexuality and sexual differences in behavior simply cannot explain the scale or distribution of HIV in the world. The persistence of the story of queer sexuality in both professional and popular HIV risk discourses, however, suggests that it must also be seen as a story rehearsed and repeated in part to ward off telling other stories. The representational politics of perverse identities functions as a *screen discourse*, masking and drawing attention away from social inequality and structured vulnerability to HIV.[55] Although the division in risk discourses between "queers" and "innocent victims" has engaged and recirculated racist, homophobic, and misogynist stereotypes *as a rule*, the primary discursive effect of this division has been to draw narrative energy to representations of what Fassin called "ordinary culturalism" and "commonsense behaviorism"—those risky behaviors and cultural pathologies—in discussions of disease vulnerability, away from questions of social structure and social violence.[56] Telling the story of queers and deviants in AIDS discourse, then, has always been a way of *not* telling the story of how vulnerability to disease is structured.

Patton's analyses of the queer paradigm demonstrates that stereotypes of deviance are not simply unfortunate expressions of bias in otherwise neutral knowledge. Biomedical risk knowledge cannot be cleansed of bias in the form of stereotypes in order to attain objective knowledge of exposure to and infection with HIV. The persistence and breadth of stereotyping in AIDS risk discourse—not only of black people and gay men, but of those who inject heroin or other drugs, sex workers, and all Africans south of the Sahara, to name but some of those who have been the subjects of stereotyping discourse—attests to the stereotype's *functionality* within dominant science and social policy.[57] Racist, sexist, and homophobic stereotypes have, for the length of the AIDS epidemic, been the necessary elements of a discursive structure in which an epidemic is reductively explained by the isolation of a virus whose mode of appearance is perverse behaviors. Following Lisa Duggan, stereotypes enact the "cultural politics of AIDS neoliberalism," or the cultural work that has been used to construct the AIDS epidemic as a morality tale about individual responsibility or individual perversity.[58] Stereotypes have enabled and authorized the reduction of an epidemic to an index of the behaviors of those who suffer it. Challenging the common sense that assigns blame for high rates of HIV to the behaviors of African Americans, therefore, is to challenge the basic biomedical assumptions underlying knowledge of the US epidemic, as well as the global one.

Moving beyond the queer paradigm, however, runs the risk of returning us yet again to the liberal, biomedical individualism critiqued by Fee and Krieger. I see this danger especially in the slogan "Viruses don't discriminate" that pops up now and again to register a half-hearted concern for AIDS tolerance and education.[59] The ideology of this slogan is liberal in that it attempts to move away from a pathologizing recognition of group differences—trying to "treat people as individuals"—with no mechanism for understanding grouped inequalities. Inequality, then, can only appear as collective failure. If viruses do not discriminate, then how else but through personal and collective failure to engage in risk-reduction strategies can we explain the distribution and concentration of HIV in certain places and among certain groups of people? These people must be doing something, or not doing something, that explains their disease burden. It turns out that "Viruses don't discriminate" as a liberal response to the phobic constructions of the queer paradigm leads us right back to that paradigm when confronted with the epidemiology and geography of the epidemic.

The second danger that I see is that simple reversals of the stereotypes of the queer paradigm potentially accede to the normative investments of those stereotypes in order to demonstrate compliance or desire to comply, rather than deviance from the stereotype's moral norms. For instance, it may very well be that black people have strong biases against HIV testing that result in much lower rates of people who know their HIV status, especially those who are living with HIV infection, as claimed in the CDC's web-based materials discussed above. One response to this would be to depathologize the resistance to HIV testing while maintaining the value of testing as a technology of knowledge, treatment, and prevention. Black people might be said to hold good reasons for being suspicious of HIV testing as a tool of public health given the history of medical violence against black people in the United States, including the Tuskegee Syphilis Study and histories of reproductive abuse, including forced sterilization, forced contraception, and unauthorized hysterectomies.[60] Thus, black resistance to testing could be depathologized even while holding to the moral and public-health good of testing as an intervention into the AIDS epidemic. What becomes impossible to imagine, however, is black resistance as a real critique of testing itself. Given that HIV testing as the new centerpiece of state, public-health, prevention campaigns presumes the ability to isolate the AIDS epidemic as a discrete disease phenomenon reducible to the presence or absence of a virus, black people have good reason to be suspicious and resistant.[61] Black responses to AIDS have historically attempted to situate it within the broader social and health crisis in the United States affecting black people especially, but also as it affects people of color and poor people more generally.[62] The cultural logic of "testing" refuses the historical and social analysis of black people, and thus must itself be understood as a partisan attack on black social knowledge in relation to which black people might legitimately resist. Similar deconstructions could be undertaken with regard to the conservative sexual propriety that serves as the normative ideal for many of the other stereotypes deployed against black people in the AIDS crisis.

Moving beyond the queer paradigm, then, will require something other than either a straightforward reversal or liberal non-recognition of group differences,[63] as well as something other than the phobic recognition of difference as pathology—racial, sexual, or classed. Instead, we will need an account of the relationship between HIV and grouped difference that treats those differences as an index of materially structured relations of inequality and social violence. Those marked deviant in the queer paradigm—in other words, those who have experienced the greatest suffering in the AIDS epidemic—are those who have been made vulnerable to disease and ill health through material processes of social structuring. Queers really exist.

Rather than the *perverse intimacies* that have been constructed as the truth of the AIDS epidemic—the intimacies of queer, racialized sex and drug use—I offer the figure of *state intimacies* to index the structured forms of violence and inequality mediated by the state that have produced conditions of embodied vulnerability to disease and ill health for black people in particular, but also other queers. Not what people do, but their relationship to—or intimacy with—the state is what structures their vulnerability to HIV. I have drawn inspiration for this analysis from black queer and black feminist challenges to the field of queer theory. Cathy J. Cohen, for instance, in her now classic essay, "Punks, Bulldaggers, and Welfare Queens: The Radical Potential of Queer Politics?" challenges the reduction of queerness to the single issue of sexuality and thus the presumption that queerness was opposed to a normative sexuality that could be simplified as "heterosexuality." As she argues, "queer activists who evoke a single-oppression framework misrepresent the distribution of power within and outside of gay, lesbian, bisexual and transgendered communities,"[64] and one of the ways that they do so is in their assertion that heterosexuality is a universally normative category. Drawing upon the black feminist tradition and in ways that have been further developed in black queer critique,[65] Cohen argues instead that black heterosexuality has long been pathologized. She asks, "how would queer activists understand politically the lives of women—in particular, women of color—on welfare, who may fit into the category of heterosexual, but whose sexual choices are not perceived as normal, moral or worthy of state support?"[66] More than simply an issue of representation, though, I am interested in the manner in which black women receiving the paltry benefits and then subjected to the vagaries and violence of so-called public assistance—the "welfare queens"—are constructed as queer figures through the intrusion of the state, even if they are technically heterosexual. If we take the welfare queen as our point of reference, the figure of queerness or deviance appears not as a relationship to heterosexuality or even to an abstract normativity, but as the misrepresentation (or phobic representation) of a vulnerability produced through a relationship to state intrusion—its violent intimacy. Cohen's critique of the queerness of the welfare queen suggests that representations of black deviance—often but not always connected to sexuality—are phobic representations of a relationship to state-mediated vulnerability.

This is the manner in which I want to attend to representations of black deviance in the AIDS epidemic: as phobic representations of real relations to state-mediated structures of inequality and violence. Representations of black deviance in AIDS discourses, like other representations of deviance or queerness in those discourses, misrepresent structured vulnerability as personal, cultural, or racial pathology, but if read against themselves, those representations do index the structured vulnerability people experience. Moving beyond the queer paradigm, then, will involve working through it, following the trails of so-called black deviance as indices for the structuring of embodied vulnerability to disease and ill health that need to be unearthed and reconstructed.[67]

State Intimacies

In the following chapters, I move through and beyond the queer paradigm by arguing for the centrality of the structured violence of antiblack racial formation in the US AIDS epidemic. In the United States organized relations of antiblack racial formation have produced conditions—social, institutional, and physiological— that have allowed the HIV virus to establish itself and emerge as an epidemic. As I demonstrate, the role of racial formation registers both in the historical geography of the epidemic's dispersion through the United States as well as in the mechanisms of its racial intensification and replication. Materialist epidemiology and its Marxist inheritance allows me to connect the health research that I read with materialist traditions in black, feminist, queer, and cultural studies, especially those connected, if in complex ways, to the Marxist tradition. These critical traditions are essential for elaborating the histories of struggle, violence, and domination that have made an AIDS epidemic possible and structured its development. In doing so, I am hoping to establish a new center of gravity for AIDS cultural criticism and resistant activism, one that can speak more clearly about the structured social violence through which a virus becomes what Marxist health scholar Evan Stark has called a "social event."[68]

My argument for the centrality of *state intimacy* in the AIDS epidemic among black Americans forces the account of epidemic to move beyond current descriptions of structural determinants of risk in two ways. First, following emerging research in materialist medicine and epidemiology, I argue that the structuring of conditions of human social and physiological vulnerability to disease is more central to HIV disparities than the structuring of risk behaviors. While it has long been known that compromised human health is a necessary condition for diseases to emerge in epidemic proportion, this knowledge has until recently been isolated from understandings of HIV. In conversation with recent materialist scholarship addressed especially to the forces organizing the global pandemic, I argue that compromised health better explains the extremely disproportionate HIV rates for black people in the United States, independent of behaviors. Compromised health has been shown to increase the likelihood that exposure to HIV will result in infection and to increase an individual's infectiousness to others if living with HIV. Over the long term, compromised health within a given population will lead to greater disease burden in it, even if this population engages in the same distribution of potential transmission behaviors as healthier populations. Instead of behavioral difference, we need to situate HIV disparities within the structuring of ill health for blacks—what black-feminist scholar Dorothy Roberts has recently named "embodying race"[69]—and the manner in which ill health increases vulnerability to HIV infection. Thus, I argue for shifting the analysis from the structuring of risk behaviors to the material structuring of embodied health as the key condition for the HIV epidemic in the United States, as it is globally.

The key intervention of this book, however, is my argument for the central role of what I am calling *state intimacy*—structural violence, as organized through state apparatuses—in the formation of the US AIDS epidemic, especially for black Americans. This is the second displacement I make in the understanding of structure in the formation of epidemic. I argue that the ill health and embodied vulnerability that structure HIV risks for black Americans are produced through racist relations of domination and violence in the United States, primarily black ghettoization and mass incarceration. This analysis departs from the emerging social scholarship on population health and embodied vulnerability to HIV, which have asserted the priority of poverty in conditioning disease susceptibility. The title of Eileen Stillwaggon's seminal book on the economic conditions for the global pandemic is indicative: *AIDS and the Ecology of Poverty.*[70] As with other scholars in this tradition, Stillwaggon insists on poverty as the essential condition in which health is compromised, leading to increased vulnerability to HIV infection, which, she argues, better explains the intensity of pandemic in sub-Saharan Africa, as well as emerging epidemics in other regions of the world. Attending to the AIDS epidemic as it affects black Americans, however, demonstrates the limits of poverty as an analytical category. While antiblack racism causes blacks to experience poverty at higher rates than nonblacks and to experience more intense poverty, as with other health conditions affecting black Americans, poverty in itself does not account for health disparity. Not only does attention to the racial dynamics of the US AIDS epidemic highlight the importance of antiblack racism in structuring poverty but also the role of extra-economic, antiblack state violence in organizing vulnerability to HIV.

Two technologies of antiblack racism have been foundational to the US AIDS epidemic overall, and especially to the epidemic among black people: the urban ghetto and the rise of mass incarceration. Health geographers have demonstrated that the planned destruction of zones of black urban life, especially the forced displacements and social abandonment of the post-Civil Rights period, provided the key human geography for the emergence and dispersion of HIV in the form of a coherent national epidemic. As materialist epidemiologists and health geographers have insisted, while the introduction of a virus into a place may at some level be described as arbitrary, the emergence and formation of epidemic diseases is not: epidemics are structured by social and political geographies, especially the geographies of human immiseration. In the United States (at least), this geography was constituted on the one hand by the forces of antiblack racial exclusion and domination that (re)organized the black urban ghettos in the wake of the mid-century reaction to black uprising,[71] and on the other hand by the overlap between black ghettos and communities of marginalized gay men.[72] Although the dominant queer paradigm treats risk as an index of behavioral perversity, and thus all those at risk understood as being like gay men, gay communities probably functioned more as accelerators of sociobiological forces (what in epidemiology would be called "signal populations") than as the structural model of disease vulnerability in the US epidemic, as in the global one.[73]

The AIDS-ghetto nexus has been determined not only by exclusion and segregation,[74] however, but by direct relations of state violence in the form of the policing-prison apparatus authorized by the "war on drugs." As social scientists have begun to understand, the extraordinary expansion of the prison apparatus beginning in the 1980s under the "war on drugs" has reached a sociological threshold where incarceration and its effects, both individual and aggregate, have become a part of the everyday lived experience of black Americans, especially those concentrated in the urban ghettos. Recent research, in turn, has demonstrated that these effects include increased vulnerability to HIV, not only for those incarcerated but for the communities from which they come and to which they return.[75] Indeed, statistical modeling suggests that between 70 and 100 percent of black-white AIDS diagnosis disparities in the United States for both men and women can be explained by the extremely disproportionate incarceration of black men, starting in the 1980s. Thus, the state-organized social strategy of mass incarceration must be accounted for in the social determinates of health that have enabled the AIDS epidemic among black Americans, and, to some degree, the entirety of the US epidemic. While poverty and the impoverishing effects of incarceration are surely important to HIV infection rate disparities for blacks, the complex social precarity both generated and indicated by mass incarceration that is foundational to the black AIDS epidemic is irreducible to poverty.[76]

Understanding the link between incarceration and HIV also helps to understand a particular gendered difference in HIV rates. Black men suffer HIV prevalence and infection rates dramatically higher than all other men, but also at least twice that of black women. Recognizing the role of incarceration helps us to understand HIV rate differentials between black men and women as being related to a gendered insertion into relations of domination. As Loïc Wacquant has argued, poor, urban blacks are dominated and exploited in a fundamentally gender-differentiated apparatus of "workfare" and incarceration.[77] Through the so-called welfare reform legislation of 1996, black women have been reorganized as a pool of highly exploitable labor, while black men have been rendered "surplus" and inassimilable to the labor market. To control this surplus population, black men have been incarcerated, primarily through the rhetorical justification of the so-called war on drugs. Black men's higher rates of HIV, then, are not an index of greater violence, per se, but of the gendered distribution of violence and exploitation directed at blacks. What is essential, however, is the organization of violence and exploitation, which *is* antiblack racism. Not behaviors or cultures, but also not poverty alone describe the conditions of possibility for the AIDS epidemic among black people. Rather, as I argue throughout this book, antiblack racism in its concrete historical form has been the matrix through which black people have been made vulnerable to HIV.

The Book's Structure

The following chapters explore and elaborate the role of antiblack racial formation in the structuring of HIV exposure and transmission for black people. In chapter 2, I analyze the *place* of AIDS in the United States as an index of the forces structuring vulnerability to disease. Medical anthropologist Wende Elizabeth Marshall has called for intervening in the *"discourses* of bio- and socio-pathology that link African diasporic communities around the globe...with *structural* locations."[78] As mentioned above, health geographers have demonstrated that the mid-twentieth-century inner-cities provided the key human geography for the emergence and dispersion of HIV in the form of a coherent national epidemic in the United States. Given both the actual and the discursive overrepresentation of black people in the US inner-cities, the history of the AIDS epidemic for black people is intimately connected to the way the inner-city is understood as a place. I argue that this geography of emergence and dispersion should be understood through a materialist frame as an ecology of ill health and disease, rather than as a geography of social breakdown leading to increased risk behaviors. Materialist analyses of health demonstrate that the consequences of poverty and social violence are embodied by people as ill health and increased susceptibility to disease, which I argue is also true of HIV. Given that black people are more likely to be poor and much more likely to live in the hollowed out urban cores, this understanding of embodied susceptibility better explains racialized HIV-rate differences than accounts of increased risk-taking behaviors. Beyond this, however, I insist that when discussing "poverty and urban health, race...is a set of social relationships...that are *prior* to the poverty associated with race," to quote public health researcher Arline Geronimus.[79] That the US inner-cities are disproportionately black is not due to other factors, but to the history of urban ghetto formation as an antiblack social project. The history of the US AIDS epidemic and its racial blackness, then, must be understood within the historical structuring of black exclusion and domination in the urban ghetto.

Chapter 3 begins with the question of HIV disparities between black men and black women. Although there are more black women living with HIV than all other women combined (188,500 versus 106,300), there are nearly twice as many black men with HIV than black women, and black men's new infection rates exceed black women's by more than three times. While the role of urban poverty and ill health, as described in chapter 2, would seem to make some sense of the racial differences in US HIV rates between blacks and nonblacks, and also confirm the *relative* sexed equality in HIV rates between black men and women compared to other US racial and ethnic groupings, that sexed equality in HIV rates is not the case suggests to social researchers and health activists that black men *do something* that increases their risks of exposure and infection relative to black women. Taking this image of black male deviance as my point of departure, but attending to it instead as an index of embodied vulnerability, in this chapter I turn to mounting evidence that mass incarceration has been central to the structuring of black vulnerability to HIV. The dramatic expansion of a population of the incarcerated has been one of the hallmarks of what Ruth Gilmore has described as the reconstruction of the US state through the policing-carceral apparatus in the late twentieth century, and into the twenty-first.[80] This new prison population has been dramatically black: primarily black men, but black women are also disproportionately imprisoned. Through a critical reading of the statistics tying incarceration to HIV rates, I argue that mass incarceration functions not only to increase and structure exposure to HIV but also is one of the mechanisms through which health is compromised more broadly for the residents of the black ghettos against whom the "war on drugs" was declared. Direct state violence, here, emerges as the key *intimacy* structuring risk and vulnerability for black people. Rather than the perverse intimacies and masculinities of black men, the intimacy of the racist state appears to be the key "risk factor" for AIDS for African Americans.

In chapter 4, I analyze the discursive construction of the AIDS pandemic in sub-Saharan Africa. In particular, I pursue the consequences that emerge from the assertion that the primary mode of HIV transmission in the regional pandemic is heterosexual sexual intercourse. Unlike the previous chapters, chapter 4 is less ambitious about offering a competing account of disease formation. The goal of this chapter is less to provide an account of the AIDS pandemic in sub-Saharan Africa than to analyze a specific discursive construction of it and the manner in which this construction restricts black materialist inquiry. I argue that the assertion of universal or near-universal heterosexual transmission, while seeming to distance African AIDS from the phobic reductionism of the queer paradigm and biomedical individualism, actually supports these reductive trends by restricting analytical attention to the health effects of poverty. In so doing, attention to heterosexual transmission obscures the ways in which the regional pandemic is structured by concrete relations of violence, from the postcolonial regional wars, to hyperexploitative and racialized labor relations, to widespread medical transmission due both to histories of medical experimentation and to the criminally underfunded medical delivery systems demanded by structural adjustment programs in the name of "market efficiency."

In my conclusion, I meditate on *what to do* in conversation with cultural theorist Lauren Berlant's warning against misrepresenting ongoing and structural violence as a *crisis*, not only by reactionary but also by progressive forces.[81] Berlant's warning helps us to understand the manner in which the AIDS epidemic has been constructed as a social and scientific fact, where conditions of ongoing, racialized precarity and structural violence were backgrounded in favor of the construction of health crisis: the introduction and spread of a virus through so-called risk behaviors. As useful as Berlant's warning is, the black materialist health tradition offers another way to represent and respond to crisis, one rooted in the tradition of black liberation. This tradition has worked not only to articulate the ongoing crisis of antiblack racism and its consequences for black people, but to throw that crisis into crisis, toward liberatory transformation. It is toward this tradition that I suggest those of us interested in a critical politics of AIDS must turn.

Chapter 2

AIDS, Place, and the Embodiment of Racism

In her critique of race in the biomedical reductionism of AIDS sciences, medical anthropologist Wende Elizabeth Marshall argues, "The *discourses* of bio- and socio-pathology that link African diasporic communities around the globe, often seamlessly articulate with *structural* locations, producing a coherent narrative in which social and moral positions justify and substantiate one another."[1] I take this statement to indicate that discourses of pathology and geography in dominant AIDS knowledges function ideologically in a "coherent narrative" to obfuscate the *material structuring* of vulnerability to disease and illness in concrete locations. Race—the discourse of bio- and socio-pathology—naturalizes the structuring of relations of inequality and domination that produce the conditions of disease vulnerability and their embodiment. Which is simply to say, race, as a discourse, naturalizes and normalizes the effects of racial formation.[2]

Importantly, Marshall does not refuse location per se. As she suggests, there are real locations or places where AIDS has materialized. What she rejects or critiques are the racial "*discourses* of bio- and socio-pathology" vis-à-vis the African diaspora that naturalize these locations and their inhabitants as pathological. But as she suggests, attending to the structuring of locations is essential; the real locations of the AIDS epidemic result from real, material structuring of life, a structuring that has a dynamic relation to discourse. Thus, in order to attend to the *structural*, which is to say the material and discursive forces that form space as location or place, a critical analysis must occur "on both these levels... tacking back and forth."[3] We need a critical deconstruction of the discourses that naturalize suffering and space as well as a critical account of the material structuring of location, health, and disease.

Theorizing the Geography of Disease

In her cultural history of epidemiological thinking, both scientific and popular, Priscilla Wald has argued that a paradigmatic narrative exists for understanding epidemics, which she calls the "outbreak narrative." This narrative contains the cultural anxiety about "contagion" within the familiar and comforting story of scientific progress.

> The outbreak narrative—in its scientific, journalistic, and fictional incarnations—follows a formulaic plot that begins with the identification of an emerging infection, includes discussion of the global networks throughout which it travels, and chronicles the epidemiological work that ends with its containment. As epidemiologists trace the routes of the microbes, they catalog the spaces and interactions of global modernity. Microbes, spaces, and interactions blend together as they animate the landscape and motivate the plot of the outbreak narrative: a contradictory but compelling story of the perils of human interdependence and the triumph of human connection and cooperation, scientific authority and the evolutionary advantages of the microbe, ecological balance and impending disaster.[4]

Wald situates her analysis initially in relation to the then-contemporary SARS-flu panic, but as she notes, the reemergence of concern over epidemic in the Western world was triggered by the AIDS epidemic, an epidemic that was not supposed to be able to happen. In the brave new modern world, epidemics were supposed to be history, or at least confined to places where the past was the present, like the "other" two-thirds of the world.

As Wald, among others, has noted, Randy Shilts's tendentious and sensationalist book, *And the Band Played On*, not only set the tone for accounts of the early dispersion of HIV but continues to be cited as a major source in contemporary accounts of AIDS in

America.[5] In Shilts's drama, a single agent (the French-Canadian airline steward Gaetan Dugas who joined medical infamy by being labeled, "Patient Zero") introduced HIV to an overheated under-world of gay sex and drug use, supposedly infecting hundreds of people before succumbing to advanced HIV disease. The narrative is a breathtaking rush through advanced-world decadence, gov-ernmental indifference, and community denial, but it is also essen-tially a narrative about contact and networks. Three factors allow HIV to travel: nonknowledge, modern transportation, and dense sexual networks. By nonknowledge I mean simply the fact that what might have been discovered and halted could not or was not because no one knew that they were infected with or transmitting a viral agent before it appeared in its advanced stages. By the time that people began appearing in medical surveillance systems with strange cancers and other indicators of destroyed immune systems, HIV had been circulating at epidemic proportions for upwards of a decade. As Shilts writes,

> The timing of this awareness, however, reflected the unalterable tragedy at the heart of the AIDS epidemic: By the time America paid attention to the disease, it was too late to do anything about it. The virus was already pandemic in the nation, having spread to every corner of the North American continent.[6]

Beyond this, of course, nonknowledge also includes scientific ignorance, inadequate sexual health education, studied govern-mental refusal to speak or understand an epidemic unfolding in its midst, the nonknowledge demanded of gay lives by the broader society, the blind eye turned toward the racialized poor, and then the purported secrecy and deviousness of those who infect others. A broad unknowingness circulates in AIDS discourses that safe-sex and other forms of AIDS education attempt—but necessarily fail—to seize, neutralize, or transform.

Beyond the moral stories of secrecy, duplicity, and knowledge, another story structures the narrative of HIV's spread: the story of how people are connected to each other. Geographer Peter Gould repeats this commonplace: "HIV travels on a non-observable struc-ture of human relation. Only after this hideous traffic has been transmitted can we observe at some larger geographic scale its deadly effects."[7] In Shilts's story, for instance, air travel is important; it is the technology that allows the virus to hitch a ride around the globe and around the country. This story about modern transportation and its role in the global pandemic pervades the literature, from disquisitions on the ease of international travel to concerns about long-distance truck drivers, and from reports on global trade networks to denunciations of international gay tourism. But in the AIDS geographical imaginary, what is actually frightening is the way that big networks overlay and connect small networks. Airplanes connect gay subcultures and long-distance trucking connects teeming global ports with backwater African slums. As described by Tony Barnett and Alan Whiteside in their widely used textbook, *AIDS in the Twenty-first Century*, "AIDS is the first epidemic of globalisation. It has spread rapidly because of the massive acceleration of communication, the rapidity with which desire is reconstructed and marketed globally, and the flagrant inequality that exists within and between societies."[8] New dangers have been introduced by connecting older local contact networks, including sexual contact, to global networks of travel and commerce. The final scene of the recent film, *Rise of the Planet of the Apes*, replays the fantasy of the new, emerging diseases, as lines on a global map trace the flight itineraries of individuals infected with the bioengineered virus that raises our primate cousins to human-equivalent intelligence but kills off the human engineers. Once in the transport system, the virus disperses without resistance, jumping from one human host to another without discrimination.[9]

This imaginary contagion geography is not confined either to journalistic convention or to science fiction films. It has been the primary scientific descriptive language of epidemic, as is seen in a scientific report on the potential role of airports in diffusing infectious diseases. As MIT public health scientist Denise Brehm warns,

> Public health crises of the past decade—such as the 2003 SARS outbreak, which spread to 37 countries and caused about 1,000 deaths, and the 2009 H1N1 flu pandemic that killed about 300,000 people worldwide—have heightened awareness that new viruses or bacteria could spread quickly across the globe, aided by air travel.[10]

Once in the transport system, the virus appears to disperse without resistance, jumping from one human host to another without discrimination, repeating almost exactly the contagion geography described by Wald and witnessed in *Rise of the Planet of the Apes* or any other number of films about epidemics.

Wald's analysis of the outbreak narrative demonstrates that even the official science of disease dispersion relies more upon folk notions of contact and contagion that emerge from mythic narration than it does on evidential reasoning. As she notes, "Contagion is more than an epidemiological fact. It is also a foundational concept in the study of religion and society...The outbreak narrative fuses the transformative force of myth with the authority of science. It animates the figures and maps the spaces of global modernity."[11] This has been very much true of the narratives of HIV's global dispersion, which seem to resist all efforts to challenge the morality tales of modernity and the primitive. From the invention of "African AIDS" to Haiti's role in what Paul Farmer named "the geography of blame" to Randy Shilts's representation of the murderous "Patient Zero," stories about HIV's travel, including within the official science of AIDS, have been at least as fully structured by the mythic as they have been by direct evidence, if not more so.[12] Against very good evidence to the contrary, these narratives insist upon describing the emergence and dispersion of HIV as contact "between innocence and danger":[13] the innocent—generally white, Western, and economically privileged—come in contact with a dangerous, disease-carrying "other"—primitive, perverse, and dark. This contact is enabled by modern transportation networks in a "shrinking," globalized world and represent the danger that comes with the new possibilities and pleasures.

Cindy Patton has argued that these two modes of spatializing the AIDS epidemic emerge from two different scientific thought-styles: tropical medicine and epidemiology.[14] Between the two, HIV is either associated with deeply pathological places or with a roving, expansionist placelessness. In regard to the latter, notice the way in which the fantasy of risk and danger tends toward everywhere and nowhere. HIV is said to "spread rapidly because of the massive acceleration of communication" (Barnett and Whiteside) "on a non-observable structure of human relation" (Gould) until it reaches "every corner of the North American continent" (Shilts). Except, of course, that it does not. Confronted with actual geographies of suffering, the discourse of contact danger has little to fall back upon except a moralizing and pathologizing attention to what *those kinds* of people do in *those* places.

What might the actual geographies of AIDS teach us?

Against the fantasies of the "outbreak narrative," health geographers have discovered that disease diffusion—the movement of disease through space over time—within interconnected geographies like nation-states, obeys relatively structured rules that are irreducible to individuals or groups of individuals. While disease transmission may be analyzed in terms of individual contact or local networks of individuals, micro analyses are inadequate for explaining large-scale diffusion patterns. Rather, at scales beyond the individual, disease concentration and diffusion are strongly structured by social organization and social inequality. Geographers have discovered that within highly urbanized societies, diseases tend to "hopscotch" from city to city, generally from larger cities to small ones, before diffusing from cities to surrounding communities in a manner that Gould describes as being like a wine stain on a table cloth when visualized through time-lapse mapping.[15] The "hopscotch" pattern between urban areas is called *hierarchical diffusion* and the spreading pattern is called *spatially contagious diffusion*.[16]

Both hierarchical diffusion and spatially contagious diffusion are fundamentally determined by urban structuring, the former by the structured relationship among cities and the latter by local structuring of relations between the city and surrounding suburban or rural communities. Hierarchical diffusion is an effect of structured relations among cities, often within the context of a nation although increasingly within transnational space. Historically, within the space of the nation, major cities developed dense, material connections with each other through trade, migration, political and economic power, and infrastructure. Certain cities, often historical port cities, for concrete historical reasons emerged within the urban network as dominant cities such that the urban network is generally organized as an urban hierarchy. Additionally, within this structured urban hierarchy, cities provide a much denser network of connections with each other than they do with rural or semi-urban surroundings. As in the urban context itself, density matters for infectious diseases, and relationship density between cities is often greater than between a city and its surrounding inhabitants. Thus, in a structured urban hierarchy, we will often see diseases appear to "hopscotch" or "jump" from city to city before spreading outward from major epicenters.[17]

The history of the AIDS epidemic in the United States would seem to provide a contemporary example of these processes. Physicist and public-health researcher Roderick Wallace and his colleagues have, for more than 20 years, been developing a sophisticated and statistically dense geographical analysis of the diffusion of HIV in this United States. They have found that the AIDS epidemic largely followed the basic patterns of diffusion connected to underlying urban structure, both in its national organization and in individual urban histories. Considering AIDS diagnoses as a marker for the diffusion of HIV approximately one decade earlier, HIV appears to have emerged in the major port cities of the United States and then "hopscotched" to other cities, diffusing down the urban hierarchy from larger to smaller cities. Secondarily, HIV dispersed near the major cities from the urban cores to surrounding communities, following local patterns of human contact.[18] The cover of Gould's book, *The Slow Plague*, captures these processes in a time-sequence of color-coded maps showing the number of AIDS cases in the United States.[19]

Deeper analysis of the abstract geographical principles of hierarchical diffusion and spatially contagious diffusion, however, has demonstrated that these basic trends have been refracted through concrete power relations. A simple and abstractly theoretical hierarchical diffusion of disease would manifest in a straightforward relationship between city size and the order of appearance of an epidemic in it, relative to the city where the epidemic initially appeared, its epicenter. Wallace and his colleagues have found, however, that the hierarchical diffusion of HIV in the United States did not simply jump from larger to smaller cities, or reflect a straightforward relationship to New York City, the nation's largest metropolis and probably the epicenter of the US epidemic. Rather, what they found was that the AIDS epidemic's dispersion through the nation's urban hierarchy was profoundly affected by

mid-century neoliberal economic reorganization and the racialized "hollowing out" of urban cores, resulting in the late-century
"dark ghettos" of extremely poor blacks and Latinos overlapping
with emerging communities of marginalized gay men.[20] In particular, the researchers discovered that these reorganized ghettos
existed in a complex ecosystem with booming sunbelt and suburban communities that were highly susceptible to disease epidemics and that could explain almost all (more than 92%) of AIDS
rate variance across space and time. This is to say that from a
systems perspective, an urban ecology exists in the United States
that ties the nation to its deeply impoverished and marginalized
urban cores, which in turn have been the primary drivers—what
researchers call "keystone populations"[21]—of epidemic. Thus, the
authors conclude, "With regards to public health, in a certain
sense, as go Los Angeles' South Central and New York's South
Bronx neighborhoods, so goes the nation."[22]

Regional analyses of the spatially contagious dispersion patterns around the primary cities of the nation's epidemic, in turn,
demonstrate that urban ghetto formation structured regional epidemics, as well. In analyzing dispersion patterns for New York
City, Washington, DC, Philadelphia, and Detroit, Wallace and
his partner Deborah Wallace found that commute density (the
volume of commuting between the central city and surrounding
communities) could account for most of the AIDS case variation
between communities. The more tightly suburban or regional
communities were bound to the central city by commuting, the
greater its disease burden. Comparative analysis, however, revealed
that commute patterns were not alone in structuring dispersion
patterns. When poverty rates were included in regional analyses,
the cities listed above divide into two groups: the inclusion of
poverty rates in statistical analysis held greater interpretive value
for New York and Philadelphia than it did for Washington, DC
and Detroit. Wallace and Wallace argue that this difference in
regional dispersion patterns reflected the social organization of
poverty. They write:

> The role of poverty in these regional disease patternings seems
> related to the degree of spread of poor populations from the

central cities. New York and Philadelphia have a more dispersed poor sub-urban population than do Washington, DC and Detroit, where desperate poverty, and its correlates of substance abuse and the early initiation of sexual activity, are more concentrated directly in the central epicenter of the city plus one or two adjacent counties.[23]

Thus, for Washington, DC and Detroit, the more-thorough concentration of hyper-poverty has meant that dispersion patterning in those regions has almost exclusively correlated to commute patterns (93% and 88% respectively). For New York and Philadelphia the relative dispersion of the racialized poor has affected the patterning of disease dispersion, with HIV traveling more closely along the corridors of racialized poverty before spreading from those corridors. As Wallace explains, while the metaphor of a wine stain on a table cloth is useful as a visual heuristic for examining spatially contagious diffusion, "[t]here is, it seems, far more to the diffusion of infectious disease than the dispersion of a dye marker along travel pathways."[24] *Specific* geographies of economic and racial domination have produced specific, regional geographies of the AIDS epidemic.

Careful geographic analysis, therefore, demonstrates that the US epidemic is tied to the organization of racialized urban impoverishment and marginalization. The urban ghettos of extreme poverty and social disruption have been essential to the emergence and structuring of the national epidemic at large, but also of regional epidemics. Indeed, from the point of view of disease agents like HIV, the nation appears as an ecosystem of welcoming urban poverty surrounded by more resistant suburban wealth, or at least relative wealth. Zones of urban poverty and marginalization thus function like "incubators" for epidemic disease, generating complex and dense clusters of disease among themselves before diffusing from ghetto to nonghetto.[25] This has been the geography through with the nation's epidemic has played out.

For black Americans the import of these analyses is to tie HIV to the conditions in which blacks have been disproportionately confined. Nearly one in three black people in the United States lives in poverty, as do more than 22 percent of Latinos, compared to less than ten percent of whites.[26] Nearly 80 percent of the inner-city poor are people of color, with black people constituting 50 percent of the residents of the nation's urban ghettos, and 80 to 90 percent of the largest ones, as in Detroit, Chicago, and Washington, DC.[27] Thus, not only are black people more likely to be poor, they are more likely to live in the areas of concentrated, urban poverty that have structured the nation's epidemic. As Wallace concludes, "in the USA the early diffusion of AIDS was intimately associated with, if not driven by, the patterns and processes of the nation's system of apartheid."[28]

The meaning of the US AIDS epidemic rests upon the interpretation of this geography. Unfortunately, Wallace and colleagues tend to describe the geography of AIDS as the geography of socially structured behavioral breakdown, reviving the discourse of social pathology that Wende Marshall warns against. For instance, in the quote above on the role of poverty in regional disease patternings, Wallace and Wallace "correlate" desperate poverty with "substance abuse and the early initiation of sexual activity." This is not the conservative argument: neither Wallace would argue that cultural pathology leads to poverty. The argument here is that structured hyper-poverty generates kinds of normative breakdown that lead to increased risk-taking and other health-compromising activity.[29] And yet, poverty still gets written back into the problem of behaviors. Throughout this research, Wallace and his colleagues have tended to explain the role of poverty in terms of its effects on behaviors, treating HIV rates as an index of poverty-induced breakdowns in forms of social normativity and social regulation, and increased risk-taking, including increased "risk behaviors," even if those risks are not chosen. Thus while this research has been extraordinarily valuable and important for understanding the social structuring of the US AIDS epidemic, situating it precisely in the "one-two punch" of racial apartheid and neoliberal economic restructuring, the theory of disease used to explain the geography they discover risks returning *structural location* to the *discourse of social pathology*.

This danger has been realized in the recent addition by the Centers for Disease Control and Prevention (CDC) of "increased poverty" as a risk factor for African Americans in the AIDS epidemic. In the February 2013 update to the fact sheet on "HIV among African Americans" posted by the CDC, *socioeconomic issues* associated with poverty—including limited access to high-quality health care, housing, and HIV prevention education" are included as contributing factors to the increased risk of HIV infection that black people experience.[30] The research for this statement is drawn from the CDC-sponsored study titled, "Communities in Crisis: Is there a generalized HIV epidemic in impoverished urban areas of the United States?"[31] As the title suggests, the purpose of the study was to determine whether the AIDS epidemic affecting the urban poor met the threshold of a *generalized* epidemic according to UNAIDS definition. A generalized HIV epidemic is defined as one in which more than one percent of a nation's general population—outside of the agreed-upon risk groups of men who have sex with men (MSM), commercial sex workers and their customers, and injecting-drug users—is infected with HIV, thus presenting an epidemic that may replicate itself or grow independently of those risk groups. Generalized HIV epidemics are primarily phenomena of the global south, especially sub-Saharan Africa and the Caribbean islands outside of Cuba. The United States epidemic, however, has always been counted as a *concentrated* epidemic: the average HIV prevalence is 0.45 percent, and it is mostly contained within the defined risk groups. According to the CDC, 52 percent of all people with HIV in the United States were MSM at the time of the study, and MSM accounted for 63 percent of all new infections; another eight percent of new infections were injecting-drug users, who constitute 16 percent of those living with HIV. MSM and injecting-drug users therefore account for more than two-thirds of all people in the United States living with HIV and almost three-fourths of all new infections. The future promises to look much like the present, or even more concentrated.

The "Communities in Crisis" study, however, found that the HIV epidemic among the US urban poor meets the threshold of a generalized epidemic. It is a coherent epidemic even outside of the defined risk groups. Analyzing data on over 9,000 heterosexual adults in high-poverty areas of 23 US cities as determined by the census bureau, the researchers discovered an infection rate of

2.1 percent, well over the one percent minimum. At 2.1 percent, in fact, the generalized epidemic among the US inner-city poor rivals epidemics in countries most hard-hit by the global pandemic, like Haiti or Angola. And given that the study excluded subjects from the risk groups, poverty itself emerged as "the single most important demographic factor associated with HIV infection among inner-city heterosexuals" in the United States, which unlike the overall demographics of the US epidemic, was relatively equal across racial differences.[32] In fact, the study suggests, "Poverty may account for some of the racial and ethnic disparities found in HIV prevalence rates for the overall US population—46 percent of blacks and 40 percent of Hispanics live in poverty areas compared to just 10 percent of whites."[33]

The "Communities in Crisis" study is an interesting look into the ideological containment that occurs in state epidemiology, as conditions of inequality are insistently turned into forms of behavior.[34] Although the study rehearses the phobic distribution of risk and pathology indicative of the queer paradigm, it also presented an opportunity (ultimately lost) for a tactical victory over that paradigm. On the one hand, the decision to engage in the pseudo-scientific practice of treating risk behaviors as practices connected exclusively to certain kinds of people who can be separated from a "general population" is, on its surface, indefensible. From the very beginnings of AIDS cultural criticism, activists and scholars have argued against collapsing behaviors with identities, as though only certain kinds of people do specific things and in turn, that those kinds of people engage in behaviors in a uniform manner. Behaviors, including kinds of sexual and drug-use behaviors that are especially suited to transmission of HIV, have no necessary relationship to forms of social or subjective identity. In fact, the assertion of "risk behaviors" as a category of epidemiological analysis, instead of so-called risk groups, was possibly the first of a series of long epistemological battles in early AIDS activism and scholarship. But what makes this study interesting is precisely the potential opened up by its phobic exclusion of the so-called risk groups. By excluding risk groups in their data analysis, the study's authors might ultimately have displaced "risk group" thinking altogether. This would have been a dramatic victory. If a link between poverty and HIV could have been established that excluded the possibility of blaming the risk groups, it might have strengthened the analysis of poverty per se in structuring vulnerability to HIV independent of the key behaviors that enable viral transmission. Indeed, the CDC could have rediscovered, 30 years into the global pandemic, the basic lesson of materialist epidemiology: poverty compromises health and leaves impoverished people vulnerable to infections, including the so-called sexually transmitted infections.

Rather than the materialist lesson, however, the CDC researchers and public health officials took a potentially new story and turned it into the same old story. The press release for the study demonstrates the basic short-circuit in HIV risk analysis, the short-circuit that leads from material conditions of vulnerability and compromised health back to relations of risk, from poverty or structural violence back to behaviors. The report treats poverty as, first, the conditioning environment for kinds of behaviors and, second, as a preexisting HIV ghetto.[35] In the first instance, then, poverty in the US inner-city is said in the report to produce "limited health care access, which can reduce utilization of HIV testing and prevention services; substance abuse, which can increase sexual risk behavior; and high rates of incarceration, which can disrupt the stability of relationships."[36] In other words, the conditions of poverty disrupt "normal" behavioral environments and access to behavioral and health counseling, both of which lead to increased risk of HIV infection. Second, the report asserts that "existing high prevalence of HIV in poor urban areas…regardless of race or ethnicity—places individuals living in these areas at greater risk for exposure to HIV with each sexual encounter,"[37] which is simply to say that the HIV epidemic among the poor replicates itself because the fact of greater HIV prevalence makes it harder for any given person to avoid exposure. All of this is true, as far as it goes. The ideological sleight of hand, here, is that while the definition of a generalized epidemic refers to a "general population" separate from the "risk groups," poor, inner-city heterosexuals are not being described as representatives of this general public. Inner-city poverty is described as the condition that disrupts the kinds of "normal" behavior indicative of the general public. So rather than critiquing risk-group thinking, the study discursively expands the definition of risk groups to now include poor, urban heterosexuals. Poverty, rather than a structuring condition of disease vulnerability, appears as a scene of social disarray and endemic disease, leading Dr. Jonathan Mermin, MD, the director of the CDC's Division of HIV/AIDS Prevention, to state, "This analysis points to an urgent need to prioritize HIV prevention efforts in disadvantaged communities."[38] More behavioral risk reduction, not poverty abatement, continues to be the CDC's answer. This research discursively stabilizes the association between black social pathology and black HIV rates by describing poverty as a scene of increased risk-taking, if not as a land already lost to unavoidable disease.

Let me be clear, however, that I am not equating the body of robust research by Roderick Wallace and his colleagues to that produced by the state epidemiologists at the CDC. The latter present absolutely no account of urban poverty to contextualize their findings, engaging in the epistemological trick of containing "race" as a variable within poverty so as to obfuscate the role of racism, especially antiblack racism, in structuring US urban poverty and in maintaining it. Wallace and his colleagues, however, explicitly account for the historical construction of urban poverty in antiblack racial apartheid and neoliberal economic restructuring. In so doing, they contextualize the behavioral environment of the urban ghetto as a response to structured domination and violence. And yet, this research provides little resistance to the discourse of social pathology emanating from the CDC as an "explanation" for the racial demographics of the AIDS epidemic. To do so requires a different science of disease epidemic than the one presumed in Wallace's research.

Embodiment, Racism, and Vulnerability to Disease

Critical medical anthropologist Merrill Singer offers a different kind of description of the urban ghetto as a context for the AIDS epidemic, one that is irreducible to behavioral pathology. He writes:

> Poverty contributes to poor nutrition and susceptibility to infection. Poor nutrition, chronic stress, and prior disease produce a compromised immune system, increasing susceptibility to new infection. A range of socio-economic problems and stressors

increase the likelihood of substance abuse and exposure to HIV. Substance abuse contributes to increased risk for exposure to an STD, which can, in turn, be a co-factor in HIV infection. HIV further damages the immune system, increasing susceptibility to a host of other diseases. In this way, HIV increases susceptibility to tuberculosis; however, there is growing evidence that the tuberculosis bacterium, in turn, can activate latent HIV... In this context, *AIDS itself emerges as an opportunistic disease*, a disease of compromised health and social conditions, a disease of poverty.[39]

Writing in the early 1990s, Singer's description departed dramatically from the phobic constructions of personalized irresponsibility circulating as "explanations" for the US AIDS epidemic in its first decade. It also departs from the otherwise sympathetic descriptions of poverty-induced behavioral breakdown intimated by Wallace and his colleagues. Rather than people behaving badly, Singer located the US epidemic within a disease-enabling ecology of the nation's racialized, urban health crisis, with HIV functioning synergistically in the context of extreme poverty, environmental assault, and other plagues of poverty. Singer describes an environment not only of structured behaviors that might enable HIV transmission, but one in which health and vulnerability to disease are determined by social conditions including malnutrition, pollution, and the synergy of other untreated infections. What Singer describes, therefore, is not simply the breakdown of normative behaviors; it is, rather, a complex condition that degrades health and heightens vulnerability to disease. HIV infection is situated within that complex environment as both a consequence and contributor: these environmental conditions increase the possibility of exposure to and infection with HIV, which in turn further compromises the overall health of those within the environment.

How should we understand this?

As discussed in chapter 1, the materialist traditions in health, including the black health tradition, understand health and disease as being socially structured. Both aggregately (in terms of groups or populations) and individually, health and disease are structured by social determinants that people enjoy or suffer. These determinants range from the qualities of the air that people breathe, to the quality of the food to which they have access, to the quality of the day-to-day interactions they experience with others. The Whitehall Study of British Civil Servants described in the documentary *Unnatural Causes* is by now one of the classic studies within this theoretical tradition.[40] The study tracked a set of British employees over more than two decades, comparing the heart disease and mortality rates of employees at four different levels: administrators, professional and executive employees, clerical workers, and menial workers. In retrospect unsurprisingly, but nonetheless definitively, the researchers discovered significant health and mortality rate differences between those at the highest and those at the lowest employment levels, with high status employees living ten years longer than low-status employees. More surprisingly, however, the study discovered that health and mortality differences existed not just between the highest and the lowest status employees, but could be demonstrated at each step down (or up) the occupational ladder, with administrators experiencing better health and longer lives than professional or executive employees, who in turn experienced healthier and longer lives than those beneath them on the labor ladder. Social hierarchy translated directly into differences in health and longevity. And this was true even though all workers had access to Britain's universal healthcare system.

The *ecosocial* perspective within the materialist tradition models the ways in which social hierarchy is *embodied* as health or disease. As feminist social epidemiologist Nancy Krieger argues, "we literally incorporate, biologically, the material and social world in which we live, from conception to death."[41] Health determinants like nutrition; the quality of air, water, housing, and other elements of a person's environmental; social and economic stress; and other factors—all of which are structured by relations of racial, economic, and gendered inequality—affect human functioning at multiple levels, including its physiological and biological functioning. This embodiment of the material and social world, Krieger argues, is a significant part of what accounts for health and disease patterns: the social structuring of inequality and violence is embodied over the life-course either as poor health and increased susceptibility to disease, including transmissible diseases, *or* as good health and resistance to disease. Both individually and collectively, then, health and disease may be described as "biological expressions of social relations."[42]

Two key terms anchor the ecosocial perspective: ecology and embodiment. The concern with ecology is meant to attend to human beings as organisms interacting dynamically with other "living organisms and inanimate matter and energy over time and space."[43] These interactions, in turn, occur at multiple scales (both spatial and temporal) and levels of organization that are in dynamic relation to each other. Ecosocial theory, Krieger argues,

> fosters analysis of current and changing patterns of health, disease, and well-being in relation to *each* level of biological, ecological and social organization (e.g. cell, organ, organism/individual, family, community, population, society, ecosystem) as manifested at *each* and every scale, whether relatively small and fast (e.g. enzyme catalysis) or relatively large and slow (e.g. infection and renewal of the pool of susceptibles for a specified infectious disease).[44]

This concern with ecology, then, is meant to guard against descriptions of environments as passive contexts for disease or health, and to attend more closely to the relationship between ecology and human biological functioning. But centrally, ecosocial theory, like other materialist theories of health and disease, insists upon the structuring role of human organization upon human ecologies. Thus the "social" in ecosocial; not only do ecologies include human social worlds, but more importantly, the ecologies in which humans participate are structured by large-scale social organization, including the organization of inequality and violence. The ecologies in which people live, or are forced to live, materialize these organized relations of inequality and violence within the built and biological environments, to the advantage of some but to the disadvantage of many others.

Embodiment, in turn, names the process of "our bodies physically imbib[ing]" these ecologies.[45] The human organism, like other organisms, exists in dynamic relation with the ecologies in which it lives or, again, is forced to live, literally incorporating these ecologies into its biological functioning. As biologist and feminist philosopher of science Anne Fausto-Sterling has argued, the seeming opposition between nature and culture, or between genes and behavior, obfuscates the ways that biological expression is mediated by the social and cultural.[46] The human body develops within what she calls "gene-environment systems, operating within networks that produce new physiologies in response to social conditions. In this view, bodies are not static slaves to their biologies. Rather, it is our biological nature to generate physiological responses to our environment and our experience. We use our genes to produce such responses."[47] "[F]ar from being destiny," she continues, "anatomy is dynamic history."[48]

In an example of this process that, in turn, "represent[s] a larger problem: a persistent inability to explain a myriad of racial/ethnic, particularly black/white, difference in health,"[49] Krieger and her colleagues have argued that the embodiment of racial discrimination and inequality explains the high rates of infant mortality and low birth weight deliveries experienced by black women. Black women in the United States are more than twice as likely as white women to lose their babies within the first year. To explain this disparity, researchers have focused on the well-established correspondence, "recorded since the advent of collecting vital statistics,"[50] between poverty and infant mortality, arguing that black women's excess poverty (three times that of white women) explained the racial disparity in infant birth weight and mortality. Attending more closely to the data, however, Krieger and her colleagues noted that while this correspondence between poverty and birth outcomes does hold true for black women, economic differences between black women did not result in comparable differences in rates of problematic births. "Bluntly stated, black women have problematic birth outcomes regardless of their socioeconomic position, they fare worse than white women at every economic level, and their disadvantage persists even among the most highly educated black women."[51] Indeed, the disparity in birth outcomes *increased* as income levels rose: while wealthier and better-educated black women experienced fewer birth complications and child deaths than poorer black women (mirroring classed differences for white women), the racial disparity in birth outcomes is greater for middle-class and wealthy women than for poor women. Economic and educational advancement made less difference for black women than white women. Indeed, the infant mortality rate for the best-educated black women is *greater* than the infant mortality rate for the *least-educated* white women.[52]

To explain this racial difference, Krieger and a growing number of health, biological, and social scientists argue that we must attend to the ways that racism, sexism, and social class are embodied by women and affect their pregnancies. In particular, researchers have focused on the ways that racial discrimination and the expectation of racial discrimination lead to elevated levels of stress and hypertension in black women, which in turn seem to lead to greater incidence of preterm delivery, a leading cause of low birth weight and infant mortality. Research has demonstrated a concrete link between elevated blood pressure and the experience or expectation of experiencing racial discrimination and other forms of unfair treatment, across racial lines.[53] This has great implications for high rates of hypertension for black people, particularly for pregnant black women, who experience much higher rates of high blood pressure than white women. As Fausto-Sterling describes it, racial differences in hypertension may be understood as resulting from racial discrimination and violence. Hypertension, she argues, "is an orchestrated response to a predicted need to remain vigilant to a variety of insults and dangers—be they racial hostility, enraging acts of discrimination, or living in the shadow of violence. Over time, all of the components that regulate blood pressure adapt to life under stress."[54] Hypertension, thus, emerges as the "new normal" blood pressure of lives lived under constant threat or perceived threat. For black people, this is deadly. Among its other consequences, the embodiment of racism as high blood pressure puts extra stress on pregnant women and their fetuses, leading to more preterm and other birth complications, more low birth weight infants, and more infant deaths.

This understanding of the social forces leading to poorer birth outcomes for black women flies in the face of both genetic and behavioral theories. On the one hand, Krieger and colleagues carefully demonstrated that birth outcomes could not be connected to so-called genetic differences between races. There is nothing natural about the racial differences in birth outcomes. And on the other hand, this analysis fatally deconstructs the racist efforts to attribute poorer birth outcomes for black women to lifestyle, behavior, or culture. Poor birth outcomes and infant mortality are irreducible to factors like poor education or poor prenatal care or drug use.[55] Lawyer Heather MacDonald may be bemoaning it, but she is correct (if only partially so) that "Kreiger and her colleagues' real prey is individual responsibility."[56] The other prey is race itself, when conceived as an essential, genetically determined reality. Birth outcomes on the large scale are determined neither by individual action ("personal responsibility") nor by so-called racial-genetic difference. Rather, they result from the embodiment of racism and social inequality as poorer health.

Black feminist legal scholar Dorothy Roberts has drawn this research together and thematized it as *embodying race*.[57] Inequality in health, she argues, emerges from the embodiment of racist economic, social, ecological, and interpersonal relations as poor health and susceptibility to disease. She writes:

> In this sense, race *is* biological. This is where many people get confused. So let me be clear: race is not a biological category that naturally produces health disparities because of genetic differences. Race is a political category that has staggering biological consequences because of the impact of social inequality on people's health. Understanding race as a political category does not erase its impact on biology; instead, it redirects attention from genetic explanations to social ones.[58]

This is where I want to situate HIV rate disparities: as an effect of racism embodied. Racism as it is embodied by black people compromises immune functioning in ways that leave black people more susceptible to infection with HIV if exposed to it, even if black people by-and-large exhibit similar or even fewer potentially transmitting behaviors than nonblacks. To extend Roberts's argument, the concept of *embodying race* not only "redirects attention from genetic explanations," it also offers theoretical resources for shifting attention from behavioral accounts of infectious disease dispersion to an understanding of the racist structuring of collective embodied vulnerability to infection within *ecologies of racism*.

The late twentieth-century inner-city described by Singer, I argue, is an ecology of racism embodied by its inhabitants as heightened vulnerability to HIV.

From Exposure to Susceptibility...and Back Again

According to the US CDC's own analyses as gathered in table 2.1, there are marked differences in the transmission efficacy of different modes of exposure to HIV.[59] While the receipt of transfusion with HIV-infected blood or blood products has a high probability of resulting in HIV infection (90%), from the point of view of the virus, all other modes of transmission range between relatively efficient to relatively inefficient as methods of transmission. Notice, for instance, that what is one of the primary methods of HIV transmission globally—penile-vaginal intercourse—appears to result in transmission in only ten out of every 10,000 exposures for the women exposed. Receptive anal intercourse, while significantly more likely to result in infection, still only does so in 50 out of every 10,000 exposures. These numbers demonstrate that exposure does not simply correspond to infection, especially for vaginal and anal exposure, which are the primary modes of

Table 2.1   Estimated per-act risk for acquisition of HIV, by exposure route*

Exposure route	Risk per 10,000 exposures to an infected source
Blood transfusion	9,000
Needle-sharing injection-drug use	67
Receptive anal intercourse	50
Percutaneous needle stick	30
Receptive penile-vaginal intercourse	10
Insertive anal intercourse	6.5
Insertive penile-vaginal intercourse	5
Receptive oral intercourse	1[†]
Insertive oral intercourse	0.5[†]

*Estimates of risk for transmission from sexual exposures assume no condom use.
† Source refers to oral intercourse performed on a man.
Table from Centers for Disease Control and Prevention, "Antiretroviral postexposure prophylaxis after sexual, injection-drug use, or other nonoccupational exposure to HIV in the United States: Recommendations from the US Department of Health and Human Services," *MMWR* 54, RR-2 (2005): 7.

exposure in the United States and in the world. And even for needle exposure, which is relatively efficient in transmitting HIV, the
correspondence between exposure and infection is significantly
variable.

In dominant, biomedical discourses on risk, however, HIV is
described as a nearly unstoppable force, and infection with HIV is
treated as a game of luck: exposure either leads to infection or one
is "lucky." Prevention, therefore, is organized as simply preventing
exposure: if any exposure might be equally likely to lead to infection, then the best program is to decrease or prevent exposure. This
logic is as true of safer sex and condom-distribution programs as
it is of abstinence promotion. While I have much greater political
sympathy for the former, the conflict between them is finally over
the relative merits of each in preventing or decreasing exposure.
This (state- and science-sponsored) folk wisdom obfuscates the real
situation.

Health economist Eileen Stillwaggon and former World Health
Organization social scientist Alison Katz have led the way in
arguing that the questions that need to be asked in understanding global HIV disparities are not about what people are doing
that might transmit HIV (so-called risk behaviors), but about
how human and ecological conditions have been structured to
produce greater susceptibility to HIV infection for some and not
others.[60] They ask: What ecologies lend themselves to successful
HIV infection, especially given the relative difficulty of exposure
leading to infection in *healthy* human populations? I follow them
in arguing that the efficacy of HIV infection from most modes of
exposure depends significantly on the health of those who have
been exposed and of those living with HIV. All modes of exposure are more effective in successfully transmitting HIV when the
people involved are ill or suffering poor health than when they are
healthy. In fact, much more than behavioral differences between
populations, differences in *susceptibility* to HIV infection explain
differences in disease burden.

Understanding the relationships between population health
and HIV incidence rates involves introducing two sets of distinctions into the biomedical common sense of HIV infection, a
common sense that is nearly total in both scientific literature and
popular discourses, even as it is fundamentally misguided. The

two distinctions I want to introduce are between *risk* and *susceptibility* on the one hand, and *exposure* and *infection* on the other. These two sets of distinctions are related. In the biomedical discourse of HIV risk, differences in disease and infection rates have been attributed to differences in qualities or quantities of behaviors that are said to put individuals at risk of HIV infection. This understanding of *risk* treats every incidence of *exposure* to HIV through a given behavior as equally likely to produce an HIV *infection*. This understanding of exposure and infection, however, does not stand up either to the evidence of infection rates or to longstanding epidemiological models. Rather, differences in HIV infection between groups has less to do with differences in *risk behaviors* than in differences in *susceptibility to infection* for any given exposure.

Both Stillwaggon and Katz argue that the immunological consequences of poverty, in particular, lend themselves to greater susceptibility to HIV infection. Poverty and other relations of inequality are literally *embodied* as ill health and greater susceptibility to infection.[61] The consequences of poverty negatively impacts health through multiple avenues, including malnutrition, stress, lack of access to preventive care, lack of care for persistent infections and disease, more environmental poisoning, and greater susceptibility to parasites. These consequences—especially malnutrition and persistent, untreated infections—lend themselves to immunological compromises that leave individuals more susceptible to successful HIV infection if exposed to the virus. In particular, the embodied consequences of poverty that increase the risk of infection include compromises to the body's mucosal barriers, decrease in the immune system's ability to halt an HIV infection before it is firmly established, and increased infectiousness of those already living with HIV. Like other infectious diseases, the immunological compromises of impoverishment increase both the *susceptibility* of those not already living with HIV infection and the *infectiousness* of those who are. This deadly convergence explains HIV rate differentials globally and nationally, especially the increased disease burden borne by black people.

In what follows, I will briefly discuss how the consequences of poverty and immiseration accomplish this increased, embodied susceptibility and increased infectiousness.[62]

Health of the Body's Barriers to Infection

In order to be infected with HIV, the virus must successfully cross the body's first line of defense against infection: the skin or mucosal surfaces. The special dangers of transfusion in particular, but also needle exposure (including medical exposure), is that the mode of exposure involves the direct penetration of the skin, thus bypassing that barrier. This is one of the reasons why transfusion and needle exposure are such efficient or relatively efficient means of infection. For all other forms of HIV exposure, however, the ability to resist infection is related first of all to the health and resilience of mucosal and skin surfaces: the vaginal wall, the anus and rectum, the mouth and throat, the penis, and the urethral lining.[63] The healthier these surfaces are, the better able they are to carry out one of their key functions: defending against infection.

Malnutrition and persistent, untreated infections, including but not limited to other sexually transmitted infections (STIs), have been shown to compromise the body's defensive surfaces. Not only overall undernutrition (protein-energy malnutrition) but also specific micronutrient deficiencies like zinc- and vitamin A-deficiencies are known to degrade the body's mucous membranes, decrease resistance to ulcerative infections, and impede the healing of wounds to mucous membranes and skin.[64] Indeed, even relatively minor deficiencies in these micronutrients have been shown to compromise immune health and resistance to infection. Parasitic, viral, or bacterial infections are also known to create ulcers and other breaks in mucous membranes and the skin.[65] Although STIs have been recognized as increasing susceptibility to HIV infection for some time, this understanding has not been generalized to recognize the role of other, untreated, epidemic or endemic diseases in increasing susceptibility to HIV. In fact, as Katz has argued, the relationship between other STIs and HIV has generally served in public health discourses to cement the reductive understanding of both as simple indexes of sexual behavior rather than generate a more robust account of what Roderick Wallace has called the "synergism of plagues," or the compounding role of diseases like STIs, tuberculosis, or parasite infection in increasing vulnerability to further diseases.[66] But in addition to their other immune-suppressive effects, persistent and untreated infections also irritate or compromise the defensive linings of the rectum, vagina, and penis in ways that increase the likelihood that exposure to HIV will result in successful transmission of the virus across the membrane.

Overall Health of the Immune System

Epidemiological and immunological evidence also suggests that the likelihood of HIV infection appears to be affected by overall immune response. Should HIV successfully cross the protective barrier of the body's skin or mucosal membranes, the health of the immune system still determines the success or failure of the infection. Weakened immune systems are less able to resist viral infection in general, and the same seems to be true with HIV, as suggested by the known relationship between immune health and disease progression in HIV-infected people.[67] People with access to good nutrition, primary and preventive healthcare, economic and housing stability, and who experience less stress live significantly longer with HIV and also live lives less burdened by ill health than those who experience under- or malnutrition, untreated infections, housing insecurity, and significant social stress.

As with the health of the body's surfaces, the health of the immune system is strongly affected by the conditions of impoverishment and social violence, including malnutrition; persistent or untreated infections (viral, bacterial, and parasitic); and social stress. The relationship between malnutrition and disease susceptibility has been recognized in biomedical literature for decades.[68] Protein is essential to overall immune function because immune functioning depends on cell replication, which requires protein.[69] In addition to compromising the body's protective barriers, protein-energy malnutrition has been shown to atrophy the lymph system and decrease the size and weight of the thymus, affecting the production of immune-system helper cells (T-cells), which are essential to resisting infections.[70] It has been shown to impair resistance and bodily responses to other diseases, like tuberculosis[71] and measles,[72] not only increasing susceptibility to infection but also decreasing immune response, leading to more extreme, even fatal, disease experiences.

Specific micronutrient deficiencies, especially iron, zinc, and vitamin A, even when relatively mild, are also important to key elements of immune functioning that contribute to resistance to HIV infection.[73] Iron is essential to promoting immune resistance to infections, but iron deficiency, resulting in anemia, is the most widespread nutritional deficiency in the world, especially affecting women and children.[74] High rates of anemia have been connected to increased vertical (mother to child) transmission of HIV. Zinc deficiency can reduce cellular immune functioning, impede the healing of wounds, undermine the integrity of the skin, weaken resistance to parasitic infections, and aggravate the other effects of malnutrition.[75] Vitamin A in turn, plays an essential role in the integrity of the immune system, and especially in the health of the body's mucosal barriers.[76] Stillwaggon describes vitamin A as a "super-vitamin of the immune system," and vitamin A deficiency as "most synergistic with infectious disease," with probably the largest effect on increasing susceptibility to HIV on a global scale.[77]

Persistent, untreated, or endemic infections also can affect susceptibility to HIV. Depending on the infection or infections, they may suppress immune functioning, intensify micronutrient deficiencies or overall undernutrition, increase viral burden, and worsen disease progression, in addition to their compromising effects on the body's protective surfaces, as discussed above. More importantly, immune responses to persistent and untreated disease provide a relatively welcoming environment for HIV. Successful HIV infection is achieved when the virus not only passes the mucosal barrier but infects some of the body's immune cells (CD4+ T cells, macrophages, or dentritic cells (DCs)) and uses them to self-replicate, destroying the immune cells in the process; HIV effectively hijacks a part of the body's cellular immune system. The ability to hijack the cellular immune system, however, may depend on how many accessible cells are present at the site of an HIV exposure. Thus, a site of exposure rich in CD4+ T cells, macrophages, and DCs due to an existing infection provides additional targets for HIV, creating a condition in which HIV is able to replicate faster than the body's other immune cells and responses are able to counter.[78] Concurrent infections, especially those that produce inflammation or immune response near the site of HIV exposure, generate the kinds of cells that HIV needs to succeed in establishing itself.

Viral Load

Malnutrition, coinfections, and other conditions of impoverishment and social violence not only increase susceptibility to HIV for uninfected people, these conditions also increase the infectiousness of those living with HIV by increasing their viral load. Viral load is the amount and concentration of HIV in blood or other bodily fluids, and viral load in specific fluids is correlated to the success of HIV transmission. The higher the viral load, the more likely HIV exposure leads to transmission.[79] This knowledge is reflected in current testing and treatment programs in the United States, which have reducing viral load as one of their aims, and therefore reducing infectiousness, by identifying and treating those with HIV infections. Viral load is also affected strongly by the other assaults on the immune system associated with impoverishment and social violence: malnutrition, coinfection with other diseases or parasites, and social instability. These assaults weaken immune functioning, which increases viral load. Antiretroviral therapy, STI and other disease treatment, and nutritional supplementation, in turn, are associated with reduced viral load and decreased infectiousness.

Population Health and "Herd Immunity"

A more fundamental difference emerges when we move the level of analysis from the individual to the population. As Katz has argued,

> in populations chronically infected with the diseases of poverty—in particular, parasitic infections, tuberculosis, leishmaniasis, etc, transmission of HIV infection is extremely efficient; uninfected people are more susceptible to HIV infection and *infected people are more infectious*. The result is high population transmission rates.[80]

The increased susceptibility *and* increased infectiousness of populations who experience compromised immune functioning constitute what she calls the "unexplained remaining variation," after behavioral differences have been counted, between those who suffer high rates of HIV and those who do not. Indeed, given the general inability to document behavioral differences that would even approximate the differences in rates of HIV between populations, the "remaining variation"—increased susceptibility—is in fact almost all of the variation. As Katz reminds us, for behavioral difference alone to explain the global distribution of HIV, "people in some African countries [would have to] have at least 250 and even 2500 times more unprotected/unsafe sex than people in Europe, the USA or Australia."[81] Collectively, the malnutrition and diseases that come from poverty and social violence produce conditions under which HIV is much more likely to be transmitted widely than in wealthier, well-fed, and stable populations, even with the same distribution of transmission-enabling behaviors. This, in turn, will have a recursive effect, especially within even relatively closed networks of people. Increased susceptibility and increased viral load result in more people infected with HIV, which in turn will mean a greater chance of exposure to HIV for those within the effected population, creating a vicious feedback loop resulting in large HIV rate disparities.

Collective *health*, in turn, has a reverse effect, resisting the entry and retarding the circulation of HIV through that population. The concept of "herd immunity" is generally applied to the population-wide benefits of inoculating a proportion of a population against a disease.[82] Once a certain percentage of population is inoculated, the whole population experiences the benefit of decreased disease incidence, or even its elimination. But we might say that overall health has a kind of immunizing herd effect, providing overall resistance to disease even if a few people suffer ill health. The immunizing function of good health—nutrition and food security, primary healthcare and treatment for common infections, safe housing, clean and safe environments, and lower social stress—resists HIV not only for individuals but for populations. It is, after all, well established in medical history that the decreasing virulence of major epidemics in the global North was the result of improvements in overall population health due to social investments like clean drinking water, sanitation systems, urban pest control, and increased nutrition. Epidemic disease was not conquered by biological medicine; its decline was well under way before biological medicine had anything to offer.

As has been demonstrated perfectly well in the global pandemic, healthy populations also see less HIV. Indeed, HIV infections in these populations tend to appear only as isolated cases because collective health provides a dampening effect on the entry and circulation of HIV within that population. And in the reverse of the disease-enabling effect of compromised population health, over time the dampening effect of good population health wards against a significant HIV disease pattern. This dampening compounds and radicalizes Cindy Patton's early observation about the relationship between the sites of the AIDS epidemic in the United States and social-sexual segregation: that racial and sexual segregation had succeeded in ghettoizing the US epidemic.[83] This is part of the story. But it is not simply that the rich and white have segregated themselves from the diseases of the poor and the socially marginalized, including queers; the rich in the United States, like the global North, have also abrogated for themselves the prophylactic benefits of generalized health. This abrogation accounts, in part, for the failure of a generalized HIV epidemic among wealthy first-world populations and, conversely, accounts almost entirely for the explosion of the epidemic among the socially dispossessed, nationally and globally. Without the socially produced biological vulnerability of profound poverty and structural violence, HIV simply could not have travelled so swiftly through the ranks of the world's poor. So while malnutrition and the diseases of poverty increase vulnerability to HIV, food security and basic preventive healthcare—the conditions of social security and relative wealth—provide herd immunity.

Emergence

Finally, I want to insist that population health is not simply related to the disparate transmission of HIV but to its *emergence* as a disease pandemic. To quote health economist Eileen Stillwaggon:

> Pathogens abound, but they do not always cause disease in a particular individual. Nor does the presence of disease in some members of a population always cause an epidemic. Random introduction

of pathogens into human populations occur continually, but they rarely lead to epidemics or pandemic. Propitious conditions are necessary for a microbe to make a person sick or for the disease to spread throughout a population.[84]

In virology and other branches of health science, the concept of *emergence* refers to the success of a pathogen like a virus to cause disease or epidemic, a success which is not predetermined by the pathogen itself.[85] Necessary conditions are required for a pathogen to establish itself in an individual, and even more so to spread beyond an individual. For most pathogens, conditions for emergence are precisely those that compromise human health on a large scale, pointing to the irreducible or embedded quality of these pathogens. In order to establish themselves in a person or group and in turn to produce disease, these pathogens must embed themselves within an enabling environment or ecology. Disease cannot be reduced to (or *reified* as) the effect of a virus outside of the health conditions in which the virus becomes active, as those conditions, and the social relations that produce them, are its necessary condition of possibility, or emergence. There is no disease without an enabling ecology and the social relations that produce it.

For HIV to *emerge* as a disease epidemic, it has required those same "propitious conditions" of compromised population health that have enabled its mass transmission. As discussed earlier, AIDS is often called the "first disease epidemic of globalization" and represented as being enabled primarily by increased traffic in people and goods around the world: the "dark side of connectivity." Historical epidemiology suggests, however, that rather than simple contact, the true geography of AIDS is the linked geographies of extreme poverty and social and political disruption: the "other" globalization, that of intensifying precarity and human suffering, which in the United States are the conditions of racial apartheid. These conditions have been necessary for HIV to emerge as disease phenomenon and epidemic. Global travel may introduce HIV to different places, but as with other, much more easily transmissible pathogens, population-level compromised health has been essential to the virus' success in establishing itself and replicating as an epidemic.

The Color of US Poverty

Given that HIV rate disparities across populations emerge from differentially distributed embodied vulnerability—embodied vulnerability as it is constructed through relations of inequality and social violence—the profound HIV disparities for black Americans make sense within the historical health crisis visited upon them. The social production of poverty, immiseration, and violence create the conditions for greater circulation of HIV among people, in part because the bodies of those who live under these conditions are less able to resist infection if exposed. This has been true for black people in the United States: racist relations of domination and exploitation have been embodied as increased susceptibility to disease, including HIV, and therefore, greater disease burden. At the most general level of description, we can tie black HIV rates to black urban poverty and its social organization.

The conditions of human immiseration and social violence that are indexed by the term "ghetto" are embodied by its inhabitants as increased vulnerability to HIV infection, increased infectiousness due to higher viral loads, worse prognoses, and, over time, far greater chance of exposure to HIV in the first place. Indeed Singer argued that the notion of "epidemic" fails to capture the true meaning of AIDS in the United States. Given the centrality of the inner-city in the nation's epidemic, the static and monofocal notion of epidemic should be displaced in favor of what he calls a *syndemic*, or "set of synergistic or intertwined and mutually enhancing health and social problems facing the urban poor."[86] Thus, AIDS in the United States must be understood within the interlocking sets of health crises that result from racialized impoverishment and social inequality, including low birth weight, hypertension, cardiovascular disease, environmental poisoning, tuberculosis, sexually transmitted disease, and substance addiction. It is not that each of these constitute individual epidemics, but that they are experienced as a global whole by the inner-city poor. More importantly, each of these health crises exists in conjunction, and through multiple reinforcements, with other health crises. The condition of syndemicity is the enabling condition for HIV to emerge as such.

As Arline Geronimus so nicely phrases it, however, in a "discussion of race/ethnicity in understanding poverty and urban health, race...is a set of social relationships...that are *prior* to the poverty associated with race." And, she continues, "the current urban environment developed under the influence of race-conscious policies."[87] The history of the black urban ghetto as a form of antiblack containment and violence may be traced back at least to the post-Civil War migrations of freed blacks to the major industrial cities, at which time black ghettos were organized through explicit political, economic, and terroristic practices. Black people and black aspiration were contained within certain districts and worn down through formal and informal violence. Formal freedom from slavery for blacks in the North was thus contained by apartheid strategies of segregation and direct domination, along with nearly unchecked violence directed at blacks.

What Douglas Massey and Nancy Denton have described as the reconstruction of "American apartheid" in the post-Civil Rights period has involved revitalizing the black ghetto using almost all of the same strategies as found in the pre-Civil Rights period.[88] The significant difference introduced into the post-Civil Rights discourses of US civil society has been deliberate structures of plausible deniability, coded as "colorblindness."[89] Whereas pre-Civil Rights ghettoization was enacted without apology, post-Civil Rights ghettoization and other forms of antiblack violence are encoded in such a way as to insure plausible deniability for all of its agents, which is to say for all of US civil society and its state. Neither US civil society nor its state functions independently of white supremacy or antiblack racism, but a verbal architecture has been assembled for plausibly denying white supremacy and antiblack violence, which is to say that antiblack racism continues but under disavowal. In regard to the structured ghettoization of blacks, the techniques of domination and violence have remained remarkably consistent, including both affective and institutionalized segregation, including racial redlining; antiblack restrictions on access to capital (mortgages, business loans, etc.); formal, political disenfranchisement; organized intrusion into and destruction of families; exclusion from mechanisms of social mobility; unchecked police violence; employment discrimination and exclusion; organized disinvestment and destruction of the

built environment; and mass incarceration. Black ghettos are neither accidental nor surprising; they are organized social structures
for enacting antiblack domination.

The analytic of "disproportionality" vis-à-vis racial HIV rate
disparities, therefore, is inadequate. It is not simply that there are
spaces of intense impoverishment (colloquially called "ghettos") in
which African Americans are found disproportionally, but rather,
ghettoization has been and continues to be a primary spatial containment practice through which antiblack racialization and racial
domination have taken place.[90] Martha Ward is both correct and
incorrect when she says, "Women are at risk for HIV not because
they are African-American or speak Spanish; women are at risk
because poverty is the primary and determining condition of their
lives."[91] While African American and Spanish-speaking women
are at greater risk for HIV because of their greater poverty (especially to the degree that Spanish-speaking is an index of racialized
inequality), Ward fails to account for the role of racialization in
the formation and structuring of women's poverty in the United
States. Black and Latina women are more susceptible to HIV
infection because they are more likely to be poor, but the fact of
poverty is itself a racial fact.

This history of the black ghetto *as ghetto* is the proper political
history for the geography of the "US inner-city" and its syndemic
health crisis as discovered and described so sympathetically by
Singer in the early 1990s. This suggests that black *over-represen-
tation* in AIDS statistics is not an index of *something else* (greater
poverty, cultural pathology, greater drug use) but is rather an
index of the centrality of antiblack racism in structuring and creating the biosocial conditions of possibility for the US epidemic: its
structural location. The ideological and discursive translation of
these differences in material life into "behavioral difference" mis-
recognizes social disadvantage as moral pathology. But we need
no anthropology of the black poor and their behaviors to explain
greater HIV infection rates; indeed, any such anthropology is ideological cover for the structured violence that has been brought
to bear on these lives.[92] Rates of HIV infection are determined
strongly within biosocial ecologies, ecologies in which groups of
people are made vulnerable to HIV transmission along what, in
fact, are rather banal behavioral pathways. That the prevalence of

HIV in the wealthier, white, middle-class of the United States (and of the world) is dramatically lower than for most black people does not mean that middle-class whites are having less sex or doing less drugs or doing either of them "safer," but that their racial and socio-economic privilege acts as a resistant to the introduction and circulation of HIV within those classes. It may very well be that for the privileged classes, behaviors are all that stand between them and potential HIV infection, but in that case, "behaviors" only become meaningful when the social conditions of life can recede into the background of existence. "Behaviors," here, are pure fetish objects that obfuscate their means of production.[93] But from a larger perspective, these behaviors are purely incidental: individual tragedies within a race- and class-based usurpation of the social resources for health. Rather than being especially virtuous, the rich middle classes of the developed world experience the benefits of healthy life conditions, conditions that successfully frustrate the take-off of HIV within these populations, even if occasional individuals will be infected and suffer from the experience of HIV.

Postscript—Gay Men and AIDS

How does the preceding analysis make sense of, or not make sense of, the suffering of gay men in the US AIDS epidemic? Sexual transmission between men remains the single biggest transmission category in the United States.[94] It is also the primary transmission category in most other epidemics in the world excluding the dominant one in sub-Saharan Africa, about which I will have more to say in chapter 4.[95] The category men who have sex with men (MSM) used to subjectify the transmission category tends to replicate the problem long critiqued in the AIDS cultural criticism of overidentifying all sexual contact between men as "gay" or "homosexual." MSM tends toward a uniform description of kinds of men, those who have erotic and sexual relations with other men, rather than being a simple identifier for any male-bodied person who has—under whatever circumstance—been engaged or forced to engage in bodily penetration that might provide an opportunity for exposure to HIV.[96] Kinds of activity are insistently turned into forms of subjectivity and personhood in AIDS risk discourses.[97] So not only does MSM tend to include transgendered women in epidemiological counts, it also includes men or boys who may have no sexual interest in men but were raped by a man. And yet, within the broad category of MSM, gay- and bisexually-identified men have constituted and continue to constitute a significant segment.

It is no slight to gay men's suffering in the global AIDS pandemic to insist that gay identity and community are not models for thinking about the organization of HIV *risk*. Indeed, this has been a standard position in the long history of AIDS cultural criticism and cultural politics emerging from gay and lesbian community and scholarship.[98] Scholars and activists battled the reemergence of the theory of degeneration in the earliest descriptions of AIDS as a breakdown of the gay male body, exemplified in the early designation of AIDS as GRIDS (gay-related immune deficiency syndrome),[99] and they have battled the less explicitly racialist attempts to describe risk using the models of "lifestyle" and "identity."[100] Whatever its failures, the critical distinction between "risk behaviors" and "risk groups" was directed against the phobic reduction of risk to forms of identity, lifestyle, and community. Activists and scholars insisted, and continue to insist, that potentially transmission-enabling behaviors like anal intercourse or injection drug-use are not confined to kinds of people with identities and lifestyles organized around those behaviors; rather, potential transmission behaviors are practiced widely, including by people who do not construct identities around them. What Cindy Patton has, in my opinion, documented most carefully is the interplay between the effort by gay men in particular, and especially white gay men, to mobilize identity and community— tools constructed in the fledgling gay liberation, gay rights, and gay culture movements of the 1970s—as resources for responding to the epidemic, as well as the ideological recuperation of these tools of collective mobilization as "risk groups" within epidemiological discourses.[101] While contemporary AIDS risk governance is more than happy to privatize risk reduction as the proper project of "affected communities," seemingly following from the gay self-help programs launched early in the epidemic, unlike early gay self-help, dominant risk governance presumes that "affected communities" are "responsible" for their risk in the first place.[102] These communities have been made doubly responsible: responsible for their risk and responsible for reducing or eliminating that risk, relieving dominant society from any need to understand what might put these groups of people at risk of risk. This has always been the slippery-slope danger of gay and other community self-help programs that have emerged to confront the AIDS epidemic in the United States (not that anyone had much of a choice): they align too neatly with the dominant risk epidemiology organized by transmission categories and the kinds of identity and community in which those transmission categories seem to reside.

Rather than gay identity and community as models for understanding the organization of risk and vulnerability, then, I suggest that we understand the history of gay men's suffering in the AIDS epidemic in terms of the relationship between gay marginalization and racialized urban social abandonment, especially as they developed mid-century. Although it is increasingly difficult to remember, as white and wealthy segments of the gay world peel away and are at least partially integrated into dominant society—made possible in part through the cultivation of sympathy and identification with gay men through AIDS cultural activism[103]—in the late 1970s and early 80s, organized gay life and racialized poverty were not separate spheres, especially in the major US cities that emerged as the keystones of the national epidemic. Gay life and the ghettos overlapped with each other not only in the bodies that traversed worlds (including but not limited to black and brown gay, lesbian, transgender, and bisexual people) but also spatially. As with prior organizations of queer social worlds,[104] the gay communities that emerged with a somewhat new self-reflexivity in the 1970s were marginalized not only in the sociological sense, but in the geographic one. These gay worlds took form, and were allowed to take form, near and next to the often overlapping, zoned areas of vice and raced social abandonment. Marginalization, here, might be understood not as an abstract sociological process, but as a precise spatialization: proximity to black exclusion. The myth of the wealthy, white gay man as the "proper" subject of AIDS, deconstructed so carefully by Michelle Cochrane in her *When AIDS Began*,[105] blocks understanding of the significant overlap between "gay men" and "the black poor," as though there were (and are) no relationships or sets of relationships traversing them. Gay marginalization and black exclusion are not the same process,[106] but they do and have articulated,[107] and I suggest that the history of that articulation is the prehistory of the AIDS epidemic in the United States.

The relative ease that wealthier, white gay men have had in demarginalizing themselves and peeling away from the racialized ecologies of social and economic abandonment may account for some of the emerging differences in the demographic profiles of white men and men of color infected with HIV each year. At least three-fourths of all new HIV infections each year in the United States are experienced by men, and nearly 80 percent of these infections are attributed to male–male sex. Although racially white MSM are numerically the largest number of people infected with HIV each year in the United States, black MSM are only slightly fewer, and black and Latino MSM together outnumber white MSM in incidence counts by almost half again. Relative to the size of populations, however, incidence rates for black MSM vastly outstrip incidence rates for white MSM (even though MSM is a proportionately smaller transmission category for black men than for other men), and incidence rates for Latino MSM are nearly four times that of white MSM. Additionally, black and Latino MSM tend to be at least a decade younger than white MSM at age of infection. And yet, all behavioral data indicates that there are no significant differences in potential transmission practices among white, black, and brown MSM that would account for these rate disparities, and some evidence that black MSM engage in fewer potential transmission practices than white MSM.[108]

Epidemiologists have begun to suggest that racial differences in exposure and infection with HIV among MSM may be explained by their different sexual networks.[109] Based upon limited self-reporting, young black MSM, while exhibiting no differences in kinds or frequency of sexual or drug-use practice that are potentially transmission-enabling, are now being described as involving themselves in networks of sexual partners that may be more likely to include men already living with HIV. Without doing anything different than young white MSM, these young men of color are more likely to be exposed to and infected with HIV because the men with whom they have sex are more likely to be infected. But this theory does nothing but push the question of HIV vulnerability back one level: what about these networks increases the likelihood that members will already be living with HIV?[110] We glean a few pieces of evidence from the research: first, that the sexual networks of black MSM are more likely to be intergenerational (or include older men); second, that black men's networks are more likely to include someone who has been incarcerated; and finally, that black men's sexual networks are more likely to be predominately or exclusively black. What it may be about black and older men, older black men, or formerly incarcerated men that might make them more likely to be living with HIV, however, cannot enter into the frame of analysis, leaving the impression that the proper therapeutics is to train young black MSM to "choose wisely," or rather, "choose whitely." Rather than other black men or older men, young black MSM apparently should choose young, white, gay men, who are statistically less likely to be living with HIV or in sexual networks with someone living with HIV.

Ecosocial and materialist analyses, however, suggest that the disparities among white, black, and brown MSM, both as individuals and as networks of sexual contact, are related to the increasing divergence of their biosocial ecologies, as over the past three decades the predominately-white, "official" gay urban neighborhoods have been heavily gentrified and (re)constructed as even more class- and race-exclusive. Poorer men and men of color may (or may not) be welcome as tourists but are no longer significantly represented as "members" or residents. These now-gentrified gay neighborhoods, in turn, have been integrated into the urban fabric as upstanding members, filled with responsible wage earners. Additionally, the cultural depathologization of responsible homosexuality, especially in its racially white face, has also increased the possibilities for gay white men to live well and openly outside of the historic gay neighborhoods. Thus, white gay and other men who have sex with men are increasingly separated from the black and brown poor, who are pushed further and further, when not completely excluded, from the beneficiaries of the twenty-first-century's "new" (white) urbanism.

These reorganized racial divisions, both sociological and spatial, manifest as divergent epidemiological profiles that cannot be reconciled under a presumed shared sexuality. Rather, the social epidemiology of men who have sex with men increasingly divides along the cleavages of race, class, and region, with poor black men and other men of color increasingly the "face of AIDS" in apartheid America. Attempts to reconcile this socio-ecological divergence within sexual identity—either gay or MSM—always returns the project of explanation to black sexual and cultural pathology, if not explicitly then by implication.

Chapter 3

Mass Incarceration and the Black AIDS Epidemic

In the previous chapter, I situated the US AIDS epidemic within the social conditions of the black urban ghetto. The populations produced as vulnerable to mass HIV transmission were those captured within the forms of social exclusion, abandonment, and violence marked by the policed boundaries of the ghetto—paradigmatically blacks, but also Latinos—along with those located adjacent to it, especially the newly emergent gay male communities. I argued that the black ghettos of the United States have functioned as the conditions of emergence for the nation's AIDS epidemic, as well as for its historical dispersion. What distinguishes a *materialist* analysis of epidemic from other *social* analyses, however, is the analytical priority of *relations* over *conditions*. The social analysis of epidemic, in fields like social epidemiology, ground disease and epidemic in social conditions like poverty or other forms of environmental assault. Social epidemiologists of the AIDS epidemic like Stillwaggon, for instance, assert that AIDS is a disease of poverty, grounded especially in the biosocial conditions of impoverishment, including but not limited to compromised immune functioning before exposure to HIV. But as argued by Marxist, public-health social scientist Evan Stark:

> At best, the association of epidemics with poverty is static. At worst, it is misleading. In capitalist societies, where poverty is constructed to preserve the private appropriation of labor's social surplus, the condition of the poor, including their health, is a dynamic product of their relation to wealth, not a function of poverty itself.[1]

Following Stark, we could say that *conditions* need to be theorized within *relations of domination and exploitation*, the latter being the true "cause" of epidemics. Epidemics demand conditions but are irreducible to them. Moving toward a materialist analysis and critique of the US AIDS epidemic, I want to return to the condition of the ghetto and attend more directly to its structuring relations while being less willing than Stark to prioritize class over race. I am arguing that, as suggested by its racial demographics, antiblack racism better names the relations of domination structuring the US AIDS epidemic than does class domination per se, though the latter functions within the economy of antiblack racism. To restate Stark's thesis: in an antiblack and capitalist society, the condition of black people, including their health, is a dynamic product of their relation to antiblack social formation, including its class effects, not a function of poverty itself. The relations of domination that produce, police, and maintain the urban ghetto are precisely those that structure HIV transmission and vulnerability.

A materialist account of the US AIDS epidemic, one that does not rely on the reductive fetish of the moment of transmission and the easy slide from transmission mechanisms to forms of identity (e.g., from a male-bodied person engaging in anal intercourse with another male-bodied person, who is not properly using a condom, to a "man who has sex with men (MSM)") must begin from three dominant demographic facts about it. First, as I discussed in the previous chapter, the US epidemic emerged historically from the synergistic context of highly marginalized and concentrated gay communities and the immiseration of the racialized urban ghettos of the major US cities, traveling along the urban hierarchy and then to surrounding commute communities. In this way, the socially produced conditions of urban despair fulfilled their historical function in being the incubators of epidemic, with the HIV epidemic being only a more recent example rather than something exceptional. The ecology of the urban ghetto is therefore structurally essential to a nonreductionist account of the US AIDS epidemic. Second, the US epidemic is borne overwhelmingly by African Americans. African Americans accounted for nearly half of those in the United States living with HIV and of those infected each year, even though they make up only 12 percent of the national population. There are more black people living with HIV than whites or any other racial-ethnic group, a fact that I argue is related to the historical role of the urban ghetto in containing and dominating African Americans. More black people live in the urban ghettos that have functioned as the key incubators of epidemic, and this is true not because of racial bias in otherwise neutral economic and social forces but because black segregation and domination is the precise function of those ghettos.

The third demographic fact, and the one that I want to attend to most closely in this chapter is the fact that more black men are living with HIV than any other demographic group defined by race or sex.[2] As described in chapter 1, black men suffer HIV at rates exponentially larger than other men (six times that of white men and nearly three times that of Latino men), but black men's prevalence and infection rates also exceed that of black women's by at least two times. Although there are more black women living with HIV than all other women combined (188,500 vs. 106,300), there are nearly twice as many black men with HIV than black women, and black men's new infection rates exceed black women's by more than three times. This sex disparity is not unique to black people—in fact, sex disparities are lower for black people than for other US racial-ethnic groups—but it demands explanation if we are not to revert to behavioralist accounts.

Black men's suffering in the AIDS epidemic presents a significant empirical challenge to *social* analyses of health and disease, especially the ecology of poverty thesis. Globally, the relative sex equality of AIDS epidemics in poor countries has been mobilized as evidence for impoverishment as a key determinant of vulnerability to HIV infection.[3] Black men and women experience relatively similar levels and degrees of poverty in the United States, which, according to the tenets of social epidemiology, should manifest in HIV demographics as relative sex equality. (I will analyze and critique this assertion more thoroughly in the next chapter.) But sexed differences in HIV rates for black men and women in the United States remain, and are quite large. While the role of poverty would seem to make some sense of the racial differences in US HIV rates between blacks and nonblacks, and also confirm the *relative* sexed equality in HIV rates between black men and women compared to other US racial and ethnic groupings, that sexed equality in HIV rates is not the case seems to suggest to social researchers that black men *do something* that increases their risks of exposure and infection relative to black women. For instance, in their reading of Roderick Wallace's geographic analysis of HIV dispersion that I analyzed in the previous chapter, Barnett and Whiteside zero in on a discussion in Wallace's work on a perceived relationship between impoverishment and increased risk-taking as indexed by violent crime rates, especially by adolescent men. Reading Wallace, they argue that:

> such [urban] meltdown [as found in New York's inner-city] adversely affected communal controls on behaviour. It interfered with people's pursuit of economic opportunity and made the adequate socialization of young people difficult. At the same time, survival in this kind of environment elicited cultural expressions that exaggerated risk behaviours such as drug use, crime and violence.[4]

They name this cultural expression "exaggerated masculinity"[5] and argue for its importance not only for understanding epidemic in US inner-cities but for the global epidemic: "Many of the processes identified in such milieux [as inner-city New York] are similar to or apparently the same as those which can be observed in Africa and elsewhere. They have particular implications for the ways in which 'maleness' is expressed, constructed and experienced in different places, and its role in epidemic development."[6] In this analysis, quintessentially black, US urban masculinity is not only key to the US AIDS epidemic but, in that it is like masculine expression "in Africa and elsewhere," has a fundamental "role in epidemic development" "in Africa and elsewhere." Thus, black masculinity becomes a key problem to be solved, not only for the US epidemic but for the global one.

To be fair, Barnett and Whiteside understand what they call "exaggerated masculinity" as a response to kinds of structurally-produced environments of social breakdown, but their analysis leads inexorably back to behaviors and the kinds of subjects who enact them. This is a persistent failure of biomedical individualism but also of social analyses that reduce disease vulnerability to diffuse conditions, especially poverty. But the assumption of sexed equality in disease vulnerability is true only if one understands ecology in a static sense—as a condition or environment—rather than as an outcome of concrete *relations* of domination and exploitation. If the latter, then sexed differences in HIV rates may index the gendered distribution of those relations of domination and exploitation and their effects, including impoverishment. This is the *materialist* analysis that I am pursuing.

Against the racist reversion to pathologized black masculinity and in the service of a materialist analysis—an analysis that tracks relations of domination and exploitation rather than conditions or environments of poverty per se—in this chapter I will explore and elaborate a recent finding that connects the disproportionality of black HIV rates to the racial disproportionality of incarcerated men and its explosive growth beginning in the mid-1970s and accelerating under the War on Drugs. This finding links the AIDS epidemic in the United States, particularly as it is suffered by African Americans, to the organization of racialized state repression, understanding both the war on drugs and the apparatuses of mass incarceration it has enabled to be expressions of white supremacy and antiblack domination. I am guided in this by sociologist Loïc Wacquant's historical sociology of antiblack racism in the United States and its materialization within the institutions of the urban ghetto and mass incarceration. Wacquant's analysis provides a key model for understanding the historical formation of prison and ghetto as successor institutions of black capture and domination (what Saidiya Hartman has named "the afterlife of slavery"[7]), their "symbiotic" relationship with each other in the service of dominating blacks, and their structural integration as a complex whole. I argue that the prison-ghetto symbiosis described by Wacquant names the mode of violence directed at African Americans that structures their vulnerability to HIV. Here, we must see the state as constitutive of the distribution of HIV and not simply as a responder to an epidemic in its midst. The epidemic movement of HIV in the United States is deeply related to the state-organized strategy of "rounding up"[8] and incarcerating black men in particular, but also black women and Latino men.[9] For black Americans the primary *intimacy* that has shaped risk of infection with HIV has not been the queer intimacies of sex between men or injection drug use but the enforced intimacy of the state apparatuses of repression: the police, the prison, and the corrections system more broadly. Rather than transmission categories, we must trace lines of racialized state violence in order to understand the dynamics of this epidemic.

Theorizing Mass Incarceration as Antiblack Racism

The United States leads the world in incarcerating those who live within its borders. In 2009 2.3 million people inhabited the nation's prisons or jails, a population that had increased more than 500 percent over only three decades.[10] Between 1974 and 2001, the total population of living adults in the United States who had ever been incarcerated nearly tripled, from 1.8 million people to 5.6 million, nearly one in 37. At current rates, 6.6 percent of all people born in the United States are expected to go to prison in their lifetimes, up from 1.9 percent in 1974.[11]

Blacks in particular have suffered the rise of mass incarceration out of all proportion. Three brute facts indicate the degree of black suffering:[12] *First*, in the course of four decades, the racial composition of the prison was reversed, from nearly 70 percent white at mid-century to nearly 70 percent black and Latino by century's end. The year 1989 holds the notorious distinction whereby African Americans, for the first time in US history, became the majority of all those entering prison each year. In 2005 blacks were incarcerated in the District of Columbia at a rate 19 times higher than whites, and DC was joined by seven states in having black-white incarceration rate disparities that exceeded ten to one; an additional seven states (for a total of 14 states and one federal district) exceeded the nine to one ratio.[13] In no state did the rate of white incarceration equal or exceed black incarceration; only one state (Hawaii) had a ratio below three to one. *Second*, rates of incarceration for blacks have "soared to astronomical levels unknown in any other society, not even the Soviet Union at the zenith of the Gulag or South Africa during the acme of the violent struggle over apartheid."[14] While African Americans were incarcerated at disproportionate levels prior to the prison boom of the late twentieth century, as of 2001, 16.6 percent of black men had ever been incarcerated, twice the rate of Latino men and six times the rate of white men. Currently on any given day, nearly one in eight black men in their twenties is in jail or prison, a statistic that rises dramatically (up to two in three) for young black men in the formerly industrial northern cities. In their lifetime, approximately one in three black men (32.2%) are expected to go to prison; this number goes up to nearly 60 percent for black men without a high school diploma.[15] *Third*, the black-white incarceration rate disparity expanded swiftly and dramatically over the last four decades almost exclusively due to the War on Drugs initiated under the presidency of Ronald Reagan and expanded during the Bush I, Clinton, and Bush II administrations. (The Obama presidency seems to be following suit, though with some minor (if important) modifications in sentencing laws.) The dramatic expansion of the population of the incarcerated and the enormous, racialized difference in that population bears no direct relationship to crime. Not only has there been no fundamental transformation in racial or ethnic patterns of criminal activity, the prison population continued to expand even as overall crime rates began declining in the mid-1990s.[16]

Rather than the "crime-and-punishment paradigm" that is used to authorize the expansion of the penal apparatuses, therefore, one must understand the rise and specific dynamics of mass incarceration as a specific strategy for governing that mobilizes the figure of "crime" as its justification.[17] Wacquant ironizes the "disproportionality" of black incarceration in the United States by historicizing mass incarceration within the long history of antiblack racial formation. Rather than being the disproportionate use of a neutral state technology, he argues that mass incarceration's racial demographics simply index its racist impetus. Wacquant writes, "Not one but several 'peculiar institutions' have successively operated to define, confine, and control African-Americans in the history of the United States,"[18] of which, mass incarceration, especially as it has been grafted onto the remnants of the black ghetto, is the most recent. He continues:

> slavery and mass imprisonment are genealogically linked and... one cannot understand the latter—its timing, composition, and smooth onset as well as the quiet ignorance or acceptance of its deleterious effects on those it affects—without returning to the former as historic starting point and functional analogue.[19]

Wacquant is not alone in understanding mass incarceration as expressing antiblack racism,[20] but his analysis is unique in insisting on the priority of antiblack racism as the key antagonizing social relation that grounds it. Ruth Wilson Gilmore, in her masterful study of the rise of mass incarceration in the state of California, situates that rise more directly in neoliberal economic reorganization, with antiblack racism serving as an ideological justification for transforming surplus land and labor in California's central valley into valuable land for new prisons and cheap but employed labor for service in those prisons.[21] Black and brown urban "criminality" became a resource for transforming surplus land into capital by selling it to the state or private prison companies to build new prisons, as well as for employing white and brown rural residents displaced in the 1970s through neoliberal labor restructuring. White capital and white labor once again produced by capturing black flesh. Gilmore departs from Wacquant in prioritizing economy as the motor of her historical analysis, however, understanding the rise of a prison-industrial complex as proceeding from the needs of capital, with racism serving a supporting ideological function. But it seems essential to me that one not underread Gilmore's attention to the antiblack racial antagonism that subtends the economic and political transformation she tracks. The crux of her argument is that imprisoning and prison-building were key to the reorganization of the state's function as it shed its role in social welfare under the pressure of neoliberal and global economic transformation. Rather than social welfare, the role of the state became primarily one of policing and incarceration as well as supporting neoliberal global capital, including through the imposition of market ideology on all areas of state activity. Race was crucial to this transformation, with state racism serving the needs of capital in multiple ways. Antiblack racism provided a deep well of animus through which state and economy could be reconstructed, and Gilmore's historical analysis demonstrates that the crisis in capital and state formation initiated by neoliberal restructuring were resolved through the reconstruction of antiblack antagonism.

Tracked through the history of antiblack racial formation, mass incarceration appears as simply its most contemporary institutional form. Wacquant argues that mass incarceration emerged as a state response to the crisis of black political demands in the post-Civil

Rights period. With the close of the Civil Rights period and rage at continued economic and social domination even in the wake of the formal dismantling of caste rule in Jim Crow and related mechanisms of legal apartheid, black people staged, and at times exploded into, uprisings in hundreds of cities across the United States, "from the Watts uprising of 1965 to the riots of rage and grief triggered by the assassination of Martin Luther King in the summer of 1968."[22] These uprisings were expressions of rage at the continuance of the racialized caste system in the United States through informal means, where blacks and other racialized groups continued to be contained in inner-city ghettos, even as they achieved formal legal equality through the legislative actions of the Kennedy and Johnson presidencies. Thus, the uprisings indexed the continued resistance of whites to accepting integration and equality, a resistance that intensified and transformed as whites fled the specter of racial integration and racial equality in cities for the racial exclusivity of suburbs.

> They [whites] then turned against the welfare state and those social programmes upon which the collective advancement of blacks was most dependent. *A contrario*, they extended enthusiastic support for the "law-and-order" policies that vowed to firmly repress urban disorders connately perceived as racial threats. Such policies pointed to yet another special institution capable of confining and controlling if not the entire African-American community, at least its most disruptive, disreputable and dangerous members: the prison.[23]

In the aftermath of formal caste rule in Jim Crow laws and in the face of black rage at social and economic domination in the quasi-formal apartheid spaces of the urban ghetto, the prison emerged as a major institution of racial rule, reconciling the contradiction between formal democratic inclusion and racialized hierarchy and exclusion through the technologies and discourses of "law-and-order."

It is precisely this "extra-penological function," Wacquant argues, that explains not only the historical origins of mass incarceration in the early 1980s but also its black "disproportionality." The "crime-and-punishment" paradigm simply cannot account for the emergence of mass incarceration as a social fact nor the extraordinary incarceration rates for African Americans. This new historical reality can only be understood through the role that mass incarceration plays in the domination of black people in the United States, even if it also fulfills other functions.

Recently, scholars investigating the profound HIV disparities between white and black Americans have trained their attention on the role of mass incarceration in facilitating the AIDS epidemic.[24] My project in this chapter is to engage in a strong reading of these findings, contextualizing them within a materialist analysis of disease and epidemic. This research is groundbreaking in demonstrating a statistical correlation between racialized mass incarceration and racially disproportionate HIV rates, but as I will demonstrate, it engages in two analytical regressions that must be countered. First, the statistical research consistently allows structural analysis to regress to behavioral analysis. As we will see, these authors follow the dominant literature on HIV risk and transmission in reducing structuring institutions or social arrangements into little more than contexts for behaviors, following a relatively banal social constructionism. What becomes important in their analysis is the construction and structuring of behaviors rather than the structuring of conditions and relations of vulnerability. The second regression that handicaps these findings, as it does in the broader literature on the health effects of imprisonment, is what Jared Sexton and Elizabeth Lee name "the failure to think about the nature of imprisonment as such."[25] Scholarship on the effects of incarceration on health and disease treat the prison as a neutral social technology that may be used "appropriately" and to "appropriate" social ends. Mass incarceration is treated as simply "too much." In conversation with scholarship in critical black studies, I argue that mass incarceration emerges from antiblack racism and is its contemporary institutional form. The racial demographic of the incarcerated are, therefore, not a matter of bias in an otherwise neutral social practice but rather an index of a primary purpose of the prison in the United States: "black spatial containment and social control."[26] This analysis links the AIDS epidemic directly to the *relations* of antiblack racial antagonism in its concrete historical form.

Incarceration and Epidemic

Social scientists Rucker C. Johnson and Steven Raphael have developed a rigorous statistical analysis demonstrating that the extreme racial disproportionality of black male incarceration in the United

States accounts for "between 70 and 100 percent of the black-white differences" in HIV prevalence rates.[27] This conclusion is based on dynamic modeling of data on both AIDS diagnoses and incarceration spanning two decades, organized by the state of residence, race, age, gender, and year. The authors demonstrate a clear determining effect between changes in rates of incarceration that began to diverge dramatically starting in the late 1970s and AIDS diagnosis rates between five and ten years later, a length of time that corresponds to the pre-1996 standard incubation period for an AIDS diagnosis.[28] This effect holds true even after "controlling for year fixed effects; a fully interacted set of age, race, and state fixed effects; crack cocaine prevalence; and flow rates in and out of prison,"[29] which is to say that the incarceration effect is not explainable by other social markers that are often connected to incarceration. Thus, the authors demonstrate that the hyper-incarceration of black men and its intensification in the United States since the late 1970s has been one of the primary structural facts determining the extent of the AIDS epidemic among African Americans. Given, further, that the US epidemic is borne significantly by blacks and that the epidemic among African Americans is probably essential to the dynamics of the national epidemic, mass incarceration is likely one of the primary structural engines of the US epidemic, and possibly the most essential.

As demonstrated in their controls, this statistical correspondence is very robust and seems to correspond to other research on the health effects of mass incarceration on highly effected communities, particularly African Americans. Shockingly, the statistical connection is so strong that the authors are led to the conclusion that the imprisonment effect on black communities is so extreme that had black men's incarceration rates remained commensurate with white imprisonment rates during the 1980s and 1990s, black women's AIDS diagnosis rates would have been consistently *lower* than white women's, rather than *sixteen* times higher. If this holds true, then poverty alone does not explain HIV rate disparities for African Americans. While poverty is essential to the ecology of vulnerability to HIV, this vulnerability has been structured by the racial deployment of mass incarceration.

In order to fully understand the discovery made by Johnson and Raphael, we must resist the danger of interpreting the statistical correlation between mass incarceration and HIV rates through the logic of risk, defining the men incarcerated as themselves the ones producing the risk of HIV. To a certain degree, Johnson and Raphael fall into this trap, attributing their statistical correlation to "causes" like increased drug use within and after incarceration, as well as the increased risk that previously incarcerated black men are said to pose to black women. They participate in yet again managing a critique of structural violence by invoking the social construction of behaviors.[30] While leaving the "exact mechanisms" of infection hypothetical, the authors seemingly cannot help but ground their statistical findings in intimations of perverse intimacy: drug use, prison sex, imbalanced marriage markets, and worsened gender inequalities. In this discursive logic, black men become (yet again) a so-called bridge population between the dangers of the prison and the innocence of the black family and community. This is a false interpretation that presumes that HIV infection may be traced directly to incarceration (that correlation equals causation). Not only is this interpretation unsupported by the statistical evidence, it does not theorize mass incarceration in the context of population health.

There are two important caveats that must be observed about Johnson and Raphael's statistical analysis of incarceration and AIDS rates. First, the statistical correlation that they discover pertains between incarceration rate changes and AIDS diagnosis rate changes, *not transmission routes*. Because of data constraints, Johnson and Raphael were obliged to use AIDS diagnosis data rather than HIV infection (incidence) data in their analysis. This was in part because incidence data was and continues to be collected less uniformly across the nation and was simply unavailable for the earliest years of the epidemic (especially before 1985, when HIV testing became a feasible element of public health surveillance), and in part because incidence reports tend to be biased toward early-reporting populations. Groups of people more integrated into public health monitoring and less alienated from the public health infrastructure appear in the data earlier, so for instance white people would appear in incidence data earlier than blacks and Latinos because of histories of medical violence that have destroyed trust between public health officials and communities of color. Even with the conceptual and historical difficulties in producing an AIDS diagnosis, then, diagnosis rates produce a better picture of the distribution of disease and suffering than do incidence rates, and this was especially true in the earlier years of the US epidemic. But in using AIDS diagnosis-rate data, the authors have no evidence tracking relations among incarceration, HIV transmission, and AIDS diagnosis, only evidence demonstrating a correlation between incarceration rates and diagnosis rates five to eleven years later. Nothing in their evidence leads back to transmission mechanisms. While some will see this as a weakness, as I hope to demonstrate, in distancing themselves (if unintentionally) from tying incarceration too closely to modes of transmission, the authors provide the more important structural linkage between mass incarceration and the distribution of suffering from AIDS.

The second important caveat that is important to note in Johnson and Raphael's finding is that their statistical evidence does not track individuals. They demonstrate that aggregately higher rates of male incarceration in black communities corresponds to higher rates of AIDS in those communities, but the authors do not demonstrate that those men who were incarcerated were also those who became infected with HIV and progressed to an AIDS diagnosis. Their statistics do not authorize the presumption that HIV infection corresponds in an unmediated manner to incarceration or to contact with those who were incarcerated. Rather, what the authors demonstrate is that the social experience of mass incarceration suffered by black Americans is connected to higher rates of other suffering, including AIDS. Whether mass incarceration contributes to higher rates of HIV or indexes a kind of social violence common to both experiences is left unexplained and, indeed, is unexplainable from this evidence. Both of these caveats point to the *distinction between:* 1) the important discovery of a statistical relationship between mass incarceration and AIDS for black communities, and 2) the sociological, ecological, or behavioral conditions that might explain that relationship.

What for Johnson and Raphael are constraints on their statistical data turn out for our purposes to be significant strengths. The profound distance the authors are forced to assume from *scenes of transmission* in the end generates a dramatically more important structural observation: *there is a correspondence between the collective experience of mass incarceration and the collective experience of vulnerability to HIV infection.* From a materialist perspective, Johnson and Raphael's discovery prompts this question: what about the state violence of mass incarceration indexes and/or contributes to embodied vulnerability to HIV?

Wacquant's figure of "deadly symbiosis" is useful for understanding the effects of mass incarceration on the health of the urban black poor. He writes:

> The remnants of the dark ghetto and the fast-expanding carceral system of the United State have become tightly linked by a triple relationship of functional equivalency, structural homology, and cultural fusion. This relationship has spawned a *carceral continuum* that ensnares a super-numerary population of young black men, who either reject or are rejected by the deregulated low-wage labor market, in a never-ending *circulus* between the two institutions.[31]

In the age of mass incarceration, the prison has been grafted onto the institution of the ghetto such that they function together as a continuum constituted through a series of social, institutional, and cultural relations as well as through the forced circulation of people, primarily young black and brown men, in what sociologist Todd Clear calls "coercive mobility."[32] This web of reciprocal relations that constitute this symbiosis frustrate any attempt to establish clear distinctions between the ghetto and the prison, even as their articulation as a continuum is meant to create a distinction and a containment mechanism between blacks and others. But within this containment field constituted by the mesh of control relations between the ghetto and the prison, the prison serves as a kind of intensification or amplification device for relations of violence, economic immiseration, and illness. The prison, as we will see, *amplifies* the economic marginalization and social destitution of the ghetto that lend themselves to disease vulnerability, an effect "disproportionally" visited upon the black urban poor, especially black men. Thus, while incarceration rates have always been skewed toward overrepresentation of the economically marginalized (demonstrating the prison's role as a technology of social control, beyond its use as a technique of criminal reform or punishment), by the early 1990s incarceration rates among the black poor especially were so large that incarceration became a structuring element of social life per se, as it soon also became a structuring experience for Chicanos and the historically dominated segments of the larger Latino population (especially Puerto Ricans and Dominicans in the US northeast). Prison was no longer something that happened to some members of the urban poor of color but a constitutive element contributing to the shape of racialized poverty as an experience.

Mass incarceration is increasingly understood as a major institution of social stratification in the United States, including health stratification.[33] While the rolls of the incarcerated are drawn primarily from the poor, especially the black poor, mass incarceration does not simply contain the poor. It has become one of the major ways that inequality is produced and reproduced in terms of race, economic status, and health. According to health sociologists Jason Schnittker, Michael Massoglia, and Christopher Uggen, "the health risks of incarceration are 'fundamental' in the sense that they may be linked to health through a variety of different mechanisms, not unlike socioeconomic status itself."[34] Massoglia's research suggests that the effect of mass incarceration on black-white health disparities is greater than the effect of access to healthcare and may even be greater than standard measures of socioeconomic status associated with health, including employment.[35] The effect is so pronounced that Massoglia concludes that "racial differences in health are mediated by approximately 70 percent and become nonsignificant when exposure to incarceration is considered."[36] As with HIV disparities, the mediating effect of exposure to incarceration on racialized health differences broadly is *at least* 70 percent, with black-white health differences leaning toward statistical nonsignificance once exposure to incarceration is taken into account. The materialist analysis of health and disease would suggest that the demographic effect of mass incarceration on health functioning is where we need to look to understand HIV disparities and their tie to mass incarceration.

How does incarceration effect health? While the direct experience of prison bears negatively on an individual's health, two facts need to structure our discussion. First, those who are incarcerated have generally worse health than the general population, even upon entry. This poor health attests to the social class from which the incarcerated are drawn: the poor in general, but especially the poor black and poor brown. In fact, racial disparities in health are significantly smaller among the incarcerated than in the general population given their closer socioeconomic status, though they still persist. And for some, access to healthcare is better in prison or jail than outside, a statement on the appalling lack of access and poor quality of healthcare delivered to the racialized poor, especially considering the notoriously poor quality of prison medicine. But the point to remember is that the negative effects of incarceration on health further degrade the already-compromised health of the racialized poor. Second, the negative health effects of contact with the penal system tends to be greater *after* the period of direct incarceration than during it. I will elaborate this point shortly.

In general, being incarcerated worsens ones health, though this is somewhat inconsistent, especially for those who enter periods of incarceration with serious or life-threatening illness. As already mentioned, in these cases, some prisoners actually have better access to healthcare in prison than outside it. For most, however, and aggregately, being incarcerated, unsurprisingly, exposes prisoners to what geographer Rashad Shabazz describes as a "whirlpool of risks," not only for HIV but for a host of health compromises.[37] Prison compromises health in three primary ways: through increased injury, increased exposure to infectious diseases, and increased stress. The evidence for each is relatively straightforward. First, we know that more than 25 percent of federal prisoners are injured while incarcerated for various reasons (from inter-inmate violence to guard brutality to accidents), as are nearly 30 percent of those in state prisons.[38] This is a highly elevated rate of injury relative to the general public. Second, intra-prison spread of infectious diseases is as much as 100 times greater than in the general population. This elevated risk, of course, explains some of the difference in HIV rates between populations exposed (in the broadest sense) to incarceration and those not, but more broadly we should note the condition of endemic infection, which—as we have seen—is an essential condition for epidemic. Not only do prisoners experience elevated HIV transmission rates but—equally important—increased rates of sexually transmitted diseases, more broadly, increased rates of hepatitis B and hepatitis C, and increased rates of tuberculosis, among other infectious diseases. Many of these either go untreated or persist after periods of incarceration. As discussed in chapter 2, untreated diseases like these, especially when experienced endemically by a population, increase individual and collective vulnerability to infection with HIV. Finally, prisoners experience much higher levels of stress, with all of its negative effects on the mind, body, and immune system.

But for all of the ways in which direct incarceration damages health, it appears that life after prison is much worse on an individual's health than life while incarcerated. This seems to be due almost entirely to the economic, educational, and political impediments and disqualifications placed on former prisoners, all of which (are meant to) impede the pursuit of viable lives.[39] Social precarity, even more than—but dependent on—direct incarceration, destroys individual and collective health, providing the ecology for mass transmission of HIV. The rise of mass incarceration has been paralleled by increasingly restrictive and punitive laws and regulations on former prisoners, a group of people so large at this point that some scholars are now calling it a "felon class."[40] Having been incarcerated precludes one from federal and many state's educational assistance programs, functionally excluding one from pursuing higher education or even completing secondary education; it restricts or precludes residence in subsidized housing; restricts access to public welfare and health services; and dramatically restricts ones employability and employment options, among the other political and social disqualification placed permanently on the lives of the primarily poor, black and Latino men who have been incarcerated. The compound effect of these restrictions and disqualifications is a deeply precarious life, marked by uneven and irregular employment, depressed wages, poor living conditions, bouts of or permanent homelessness, and highly elevated stress. The permanent stigma of incarceration and its function in ongoing state disqualification produces greater ill health and disease for those who have been incarcerated.

The individual perspective is only part of the picture. In thinking about mass incarceration as a technology of social and health stratification, we must remember that prisoners and former prisoners are "embedded" in social worlds, as member of families, neighborhoods, and communities, all of whom are affected by the disruptions of incarceration and the long-term disabilities placed on those who have been incarcerated. Particularly in those communities most affected by mass incarceration—the black, urban poor—where up to 15 percent of all adults in the community may be incarcerated at any given time, and where up to 60 percent of all men in the community may either be or have been incarcerated, the social and economic effects of incarceration spill over into the broader community, in what scholars euphemistically describe as "collateral damage" or "unintended consequences."[41] Mass incarceration, precisely in its *mass*, brings down the quality of life of those most effected by it. It increases and intensifies the social and economic precarity that constitute the ecology of health and disease from which the incarcerated are drawn and to which they return.[42] Rather than a "separate sphere" of risk and behaviors, the prison functions as an intensification or amplification mechanism within the ecology of precarity lived by the black, urban poor, making life more precarious, more poor, more ill, more violent, and more stressful. Mass incarceration makes the conditions of living and the conditions of health worse, which may in fact be its primary function.

As stated earlier, these effects on health, both individual and collective, account for as much as 70 percent of black-white health disparities. The size of this mediating effect is due primarily to the extraordinary disproportionality of mass incarceration. While health effects like these are not ruled by simple cause-and-effect, given that population dynamics are systemic, recursive, and ecological, blunt facts still tell us a large part of the story: racial disparities in health index racial disparities in incarceration. In other words, African Americans have worse health in part (potentially a large part) because so many more are or have been incarcerated. This effect is not simply additive but compounding and exponential. But in addition to the blunt fact of quantity, there is also reason to believe that the qualities of incarceration are different for blacks and whites in ways that amplify even further the quantitative effects. There is, of course, a significant literature on the differences between doing "black time" versus "white time" in prison, with "black time" marked by much harsher treatment from the agencies of the state in all of its guises, from judges and juries, to prison guards, parole boards, and physical- and mental-health professionals. While to my knowledge no direct research has been done to examine the specific health effects of antiblack violence directed at the incarcerated, it is fair to speculate that the greater violence directed at African Americans weighs on their health in prison and beyond it. We do know, however, that African Americans are more likely than whites to be incarcerated in prisons than in local jails. As sociologists Marc Mauer and Ryan King note, "Since jail stays are relatively short compared to prison terms, the collateral consequences of incarceration—separation from family, reduced employment prospects—are generally less severe than for persons spending a year or more in state prison."[43] Thus, there is good reason to suspect that the qualities of incarceration as meted out to blacks versus whites plays some additional role in health disparities, though researchers agree that quantity plays the dominant role.

It is through its function as an institution of social, economic, and health stratification that I want to insist that the prison plays its primary role in the AIDS epidemic for African Americans, and therefore in the US national epidemic. Breaking from the logic of risk and theorizing HIV prevalence and transmission in terms of structurally mediated ecologies of health demands an account of the material relations and socio-ecological conditions that structure health for African Americans.[44] Mass incarceration turns out to be essential to the construction and replication of that social and health ecology, but not only or primarily as a scene of risk, behaviors, and direct transmission. Rather, mass incarceration is a fundamental institution through which the condition for illness and disease—their ecology—are produced for African Americans, including deepened poverty but not reducible to it. Its effect, in turn, is anything but marginal, accounting for 70 percent or more of the health difference and HIV rate differences between blacks and whites. Which is to say that mass incarceration is *fundamental*, in two senses: not just as an institution for producing inequality and embodied vulnerability to HIV, but as one of the most important.

It is important, then, not to treat "the prison" as the scene of risk behaviors—with all of the salaciousness that scene invokes in the new age of prison pornography—but to think of mass incarceration in its symbiosis with the urban ghetto as a technology or apparatus that produces effects in the health of populations. In this case, the deadly symbiosis of mass incarceration and the black ghetto degrades the overall health of those captured within its continuum by structuring and deepening racial and classed inequality, damaging the health of the incarcerated over their lifetimes (even if not always while incarcerated), increasing and concentrating the possibilities of exposure to HIV and other transmissible diseases, and decreasing the overall health of those communities from which the incarcerated are captured and to which they are released.[45] In each of these modes, and especially in their interarticulation, mass incarceration functions as an active technology for producing ill health and vulnerability to disease, including HIV, in communities of black urban poverty, the communities most thoroughly articulated into the apparatuses of mass incarceration. As mass incarceration has intensified and expanded over the last four decades, so has this social and physiological vulnerability of the ghetto, indexing almost exactly the organization of the US AIDS epidemic as an affliction visited upon the black poor. This deadly symbiosis has functioned in a complex way as a technology of power, structuring zones of black life as zones of slow death[46] and forming African Americans as a precarious population with greatly increased vulnerability to HIV. The speed-up in this vulnerability, as registered in incidence and prevalence data, suggests, in turn, that even within zones of slow death, some deaths happen slower—or faster—than others.

Gendering Racial Domination and AIDS

At the beginning of this chapter, I argued that the gendered difference in HIV rates between black men and women posed a challenge to materialist accounts of epidemic, especially those that attempt to ground disease vulnerability in the ecology of poverty. Treating poverty as a static condition that increases embodied vulnerability to HIV has few resources for understanding differences within that context, especially differences that appear so clearly as gender, leading researchers and others to gender as the explanation. Thus, black men's increased HIV rates are explained in terms of black masculinity.

Against this reading, I have argued that black men's HIV rates are better understood as the consequence of the *violent intimacy of the racist state.* One of the effects of racialized mass incarceration, itself an expression of antiblack racial formation in this historical instance, has been greatly increased exposure and vulnerability to HIV, an effect that explains all or nearly all of the rate disparities between black and white men. It also explains all or nearly all of the rate disparities between black and white women. Given the enormity of these rate disparities and the degree to which AIDS is a black epidemic in the United States, mass incarceration must be understood as not only essential to the understanding of AIDS for black Americans but also for all Americans.

Before closing, however, I want to again enfold mass incarceration into the dynamics of antiblack racism as a complex historical whole in order to ward against collapsing black women's experience into an effect of black men's. Johnson and Raphael make a compelling statistical argument for understanding black women's AIDS rates in the context of black men's incarceration rates. In fact, they pursue regression analyses that seem to demonstrate that black women's incarceration rates have not significantly affected their HIV rates, or at least not in ways that are not overwhelmed in the statistical data by the sheer magnitude of black men's imprisonment.[47] It thus appears that black women's experience with HIV is a reflection of the state violence directed first at black men. This is true, however, only if we separate mass incarceration from the other technologies of racial domination directed at black people and experienced as a complex whole. Whereas I have been discussing mass incarceration in relation to social exclusion in the figure of the "deadly symbiosis" between prison and ghetto, scholars of race and gender have argued for a third form of domination directed primarily at black women that has structured and worsened the lives of the urban poor: welfare, especially as it has been reorganized into "workfare" after the 1996 Welfare Reform Act.

Wacquant describes a triangulated "problematic linking urban marginality, welfare policy, and punishment."[48] The "uniquely rigid ethnoracial cleavage that isolates African Americans in physical, social and symbolic space" in the United States "intensifies class decomposition at the bottom, facilitates the shift to workfare, and escalates the rolling out of the penal state."[49] Thus, mass incarceration as an expression of the antiblack penal state exists in concert with the shift in "assistential" discipline from welfare to workfare "according to a gendered division of labor, the men being handled by [the state's] penal wing while (their) women and children are managed by a revamped welfare-workfare system designed to buttress casual employment,"[50] with the overall effect being "intensifie[d] class decomposition at the bottom." This is the precise description of the formation and regulation of the black urban ghetto: racial exclusion, "law and order" state violence, and hyperexploitation through workfare-ization.

In that the transformation of welfare has made poor women's lives more precarious, it has surely increased their vulnerability to HIV. We know, for instance, that women who disappeared from welfare rolls after 1996 were as likely to have simply "disappeared" into homelessness or already overstretched networks of familial and communal support as to have found employment, and that workfare has increased the vulnerability experienced by women working in it, given that their assistance is tied to their "flexibility" as labor.[51] The increased stress, decreased assistance, and altogether heightened precarity, in turn, have worsened the social and ecological conditions of the urban ghetto—"decomposition at the bottom"—contributing to the intensification of conditions of embodied vulnerability to illness and disease that I have also suggested come with mass incarceration. All of this explains the dramatic epidemic rate disparities between blacks and nonblacks.

The gendered difference between black men's and women's HIV rates index their gendered insertion into this triangulated assault. While black men and women are as blacks segregated into ghettos, the relations of domination and exploitation directed at ghettos are essentially if not exclusively gendered. Black men's insertion into the penal apparatuses of antiblack domination have been especially important in heightening exposure and vulnerability to HIV, but this takes place in the context of a triangulated and gender-differentiated assault on African Americans and, I argue, makes no sense outside of that context. Black men's higher HIV rates, then, are not an index of greater violence per se, but of the gendered distribution of violence and exploitation directed at black people. What is essential, however, is the whole in relation to which the parts are articulated.

A materialist analysis of epidemic situates disease within *relations* of domination and exploitation. Working within this tradition, I have argued for an account of AIDS that locates it within the historically specific organization of relations of antiblack domination that have been contemporary with the epidemic: the web of force relations enclosing and connecting the black urban ghetto and the prison. The black ghetto of the United States is insufficiently understood as an "ecology of poverty." It is, rather, the scene of direct relations of state violence through which blacks have been made especially vulnerable to exposure and susceptible to infection with HIV. Neither behaviors nor condition, but relations of antiblack domination organized through the state have structured exposure and vulnerability to HIV in the United States, especially for those of the black diaspora in relation to whom those relations of force have been directed. That black people suffer "disproportionately" from relations of violence directed precisely against them is no surprise.

Chapter 4

Representing Global AIDS: Africa, Heterosexuality, Violence

Recent and emerging scholarship and discourses on the global AIDS pandemic have insisted upon privileging the perspective of sub-Saharan Africa, the so-called global epicenter, in descriptions of it. For instance, medical anthropologist and physician Didier Fassin, in asking whether the epidemic of South Africa is exemplary of the forces structuring the global pandemic or of a unique form, captures the sense in which "African AIDS" is increasingly being understood as paradigmatic. He writes, "Uniqueness *or* exemplarity? Such seems also to be the dialectic involved in understanding the situation of AIDS in South Africa. Once again, the epidemiological as well as political evidence appears to oscillate between exceptionalism...and extremism."[1] Fassin answers, however, that the "contradiction is only apparent."[2] South Africa is both exemplary and unique, he asserts, as its uniqueness lies fundamentally in the extremity of the structural forces that are common to the organization of pandemic on a global scale, an extremity that emerges from what Fassin characterizes as the uniqueness of the apartheid system in maintaining and deepening the racist inequality, poverty, and dislocation that exist elsewhere in less intense, if still catastrophic forms. "It is possible," he writes, "to think simultaneously of the historical exceptionalism of South African AIDS, as the product of apartheid, *and* its structural extremism, as a radical expression of phenomena observed elsewhere."[3] South African apartheid was a unique, political and economic, racial formation, but it was also but a "radical expression of phenomena observed elsewhere" in the formation of the global pandemic. And whereas South Africa is the most radical example, sub-Saharan Africa at large is itself being (re)constructed as both unique and exemplary of the global pandemic: the most extreme version of conditions that organize and structure the global pandemic, per se.

I have learned a great deal from much of this scholarship. The extraordinary "democracy of suffering" found in the sub-Saharan experience with AIDS has been an important point of counterarticulation to the exoticizing dismissal of the queer paradigm and its hold on dominant knowledge in the United States and in official global institutions. Although both historical and current scholarship and public discourses have tried to describe the African pandemic as emerging from exotic practices, Africans and Africanists continue to respond that the depth and breadth of their pandemic indexes less any kind of sexual deviance than the racist brutality of the postcolony under global capital.[4] Africanist scholars have taught me, especially, to see the ecologies of health and disease that underlie epidemic or prevent it. But as I have come to learn the lessons of Africanist scholars, and as I have brought them to reflect upon the US epidemic and its racial burden, I have been struck by the ways that the scholarship that has oriented itself to the experience of sub-Saharan Africa falls short when brought to the black American experience. This discontinuity has prompted me to question the representation of sub-Saharan Africa that is emerging in the scholarship and public discourses. If, as Fassin suggests, sub-Saharan Africa is exemplary of the forces organizing the global pandemic—unique only in its severity—then what is being put forth as descriptive of sub-Saharan Africa?

Those interested in a critical account and critical politics of AIDS are confronted by the fact that the global burden of the pandemic is felt disproportionately by Africans south of the Sahara and the peoples of the larger African diaspora. More than half of all people living with Human Immunodeficiency Virus (HIV) in the world live in the nations of sub-Saharan Africa, as do two-thirds of all women, even though the people of this region account for only ten percent of the world's population.[5] Outside of sub-Saharan Africa, the nations with the greatest prevalence rates are the Caribbean island nations, excluding Cuba: the former plantation economies of the Middle Passage and currently subject to US imperial power. The parallelism with the United States is striking: it seems that sub-Saharan Africa and the greater African diaspora suffer disease, mortality, and violence much like America's black ghettos, with almost exactly parallel AIDS epidemics. Indeed, as in the United States, to talk about women and AIDS globally is to talk about black women.

Or not. Scholarship on the global pandemic routinely and insistently draws upon but then obfuscates the suffering of the people of the African diaspora. For instance, absolutely no analysis of racism appears in Colleen O'Manique's *Neoliberalism and AIDS epidemic in Sub-Saharan Africa*, her otherwise very important book on the colonial history and contemporary, neocolonial structuring of the conditions of impoverishment and gendered inequality that have helped propel the AIDS epidemic in sub-Saharan Africa.[6] The term "racism" has three entries in the book's index: the first to a page in which neither the word nor the concept seem to appear, the second to a quotation from another author, and the third to racist representations in scientific and popular accounts of African sexual behaviors. Neither colonialism nor neoliberalism are represented as being significantly racial projects. Similarly, Eileen Stillwaggon's masterful study of what she calls the "ecology of poverty" conditioning vulnerability to HIV in sub-Saharan Africa provides an excellent analysis of the role of representation in the history of scholarship on the regional pandemic, but she seems completely unable to make a connection between those representations and the ecology of poverty that she finds.[7] Racist representations have been a way of *not* seeing ecological conditions but seem to have no connection to the formation of those conditions for Stillwaggon. Or again, the groundbreaking collection *Women, Poverty, and AIDS: Sex, Drugs, and Structural Violence*, first published in the mid-1990s and reissued in 2011, only discusses racism to the degree that it is said to increase women's poverty—racism thus being conceived as a form of bias in otherwise race-neutral economic processes—and quickly drops out of the analysis, even at the level of language.[8] As Paul Farmer and Jim Yong Kim write in their introduction, "These women [with AIDS] are not of the same 'race' or ethnic background. In fact, what they have in common is almost exclusively their poverty and their gender."[9] This, even though 60 percent of all women in the United States living with AIDS are black, as are at least 60 percent of all women globally. Thus, in the critical scholarship black becomes nonwhite, and then simply poor, with all questions of racism, and especially antiblack racism, quietly disappeared. The extreme suffering of black people is appropriated to other ends, ends that confuse the specificity of antiblack racism in structuring vulnerability to disease. The global "fact of blackness"[10] is then recognized—to the degree that recognition is involved—only within racist speech, where the effects of antiblack racist violence and inequality are ideologically naturalized as the biological or cultural traits of black people, against which the liberal, "colorblind" discourses on AIDS are routinely stopped short.

In this chapter, I analyze the discursive construction of the AIDS pandemic in sub-Saharan Africa. In particular, I am interested in the consequences that emerge from the assertion that the primary mode of HIV transmission in the regional pandemic is heterosexual sexual intercourse. Heterosexual transmission as a framing device in discourses on the AIDS pandemic in sub-Saharan Africa is a dominant, though not universal, trend; scholars and activists have initiated structural arguments about the regional pandemic in other ways. But with the exception of those who challenge universal heterosexuality in Africa and in its pandemic (often in the name of gay, lesbian, bisexual, transgendered, and otherwise queer Africans), this narrative frame is often evident at least as a background presumption in both scholarship and political discourses. That it is so persistent suggests that it does important discursive work. As I demonstrate, the assertion of universal or near-universal heterosexual transmission, while seeming to distance African AIDS from the phobic reductionism of the queer paradigm and biomedical individualism, actually supports these reductive trends by restricting analytical attention to the health effects of poverty. In so doing, attention to heterosexual transmission obscures the ways in which the regional pandemic is structured by concrete relations of violence, from the postcolonial regional wars, to hyperexploitative and racialized labor relations, to widespread medical transmission due both to histories of medical experimentation and to the criminally underfunded medical delivery systems demanded by structural adjustment programs in the name of "market efficiency." Relations of domination and violence come into visibility as relatively static conditions, and the force of antiblack racism seems to disappear.

The goal of this chapter is less to provide an account of the AIDS pandemic in sub-Saharan Africa than to analyze a specific discursive construction of it. Unlike the previous chapters, this chapter is less ambitious about offering a competing account of disease formation. Instead, my contribution here is to deconstruct representations of the African pandemic and the manner in which they restrict black materialist inquiry. Near the end of the chapter, I do champion some potential lines of investigation based upon current scholarship, but anything further is beyond the capacity of this book and its author. But I hope that by reactivating and updating a tradition of scholarship critical of the discursive construction of "African AIDS," including its presumed heterosexuality, I may not only empower kinds of scholarship that attend more closely to the relationship between the AIDS pandemic and the material structuring of violence—racial, economic, gendered, and sexual—but also further challenge the reduction of structural location to black racial pathology that seems to be one of the endlessly renewable resources of AIDS discourse.[11]

The Sexual Politics of African AIDS

The epidemiological profile of the regional pandemic in sub-Saharan Africa is said to be different. With only a few local exceptions, sub-Saharan Africa is the only region in the world in which women's HIV rates have consistently equaled or exceeded men's. In almost all other national epidemics, HIV rates for men exceed those of women, often overwhelmingly. While restricted categories of women may have high rates of HIV, men suffer much higher rates of HIV at the scales of nation or region. This has not been the case in sub-Saharan Africa. From the very earliest epidemiological descriptions, sub-Saharan Africa has been understood as unique or different for its relative gendered equality in disease prevalence and, in general, the disproportionately feminine incidence rates. While the earliest estimates suggested that men outnumbered women with HIV (though not by the overwhelming disparities found in other places), recent estimates suggest that women now constitute the definitive majority of those living with HIV and of those infected with HIV each year.

The uniquely equalitarian or feminine profile of suffering in sub-Saharan Africa has long been attributed to the predominance of heterosexual transmission, which again, has been globally unique. In no other region of the world has heterosexual transmission been understood to be the dominant mode of transmission. Indeed, "African AIDS" has been represented as almost entirely a heterosexual epidemic. For instance, O'Manique declares confidently:

> A significant difference between the "western" epidemic and the emerging epidemics in the "Third World" was the roughly equal numbers of males and females infected in the Third World. In Africa, heterosexual transmission was estimated to account for between 80 and 90 per cent of all cases, the other 20 per cent, a combination of perinatal transmissions and infections through contaminated blood.[12]

O'Manique follows others in suggesting not only that heterosexual transmission has been significant in the sub-Saharan pandemic, but that it has been nearly exclusive. Notice that her numbers add up to no same-sex sexuality or drug use in the African pandemic.

Marc Epprecht has argued that this scholarly and political insistence on the exclusivity of heterosexuality in "African AIDS" rests not only on colonialist science but on the racist fantasy of a singular African sexuality.[13] As he notes, the heterosexuality of the African pandemic is now so taken for granted that scholars assert it without bothering to offer even a citation, let alone concrete evidence.[14] But as Epprecht argues, this common sense depends not only on the studied refusal to acknowledge African homosexualities but also on dangerously colonialist forms of anthropological investigation. Universal heterosexuality has been established in Africa without any scientific basis or at best, the most unreflexive ethnography and behavioral investigation, with little or no effort to account for linguistic or cultural difference. Behavioral and ethnographic scholars have failed to attend to different ways of organizing sexual identity, to attend to the political, moral, and emotional stakes of admitting same-sex sexualities, or to interrogate the very category of "sex." While Western scholars and health activists may have a broad understanding of what might count as "sex" between people, Epprecht demonstrates that in multiple African cultures, erotic contact that exceeds purely reproductive (or potentially reproductive) vaginal intercourse is not called "sex." This is not to say that it is absent, but that it is not conceptually organized under the category "sex." Nonreproductive activities and arrangements, he demonstrates, do "not necessarily fall within that definition [of 'sex'] but ha[ve] their own distinct terms or euphemisms."[15] This linguistic and cultural difference in conceptualizing erotic contact seriously calls into question the routine behavioral surveys used throughout the continent that ask for personal histories of same-sex "sex" and its role in transmitting HIV. Beyond the presumption that people want to, or are free to, share their intimate histories, these surveys presume a shared understanding of erotic behavior that is not, in fact, shared.

Epprecht argues that the ideological insistence upon heterosexuality in accounts of the African pandemic is consistent with a long history of colonialist and racist anthropology that has purported to find singular "African sexuality" marked by its overall deviance and exoticism. He writes:

> This hypothetical singular African sexuality includes, above all, the supposed nonexistence of homosexuality or bisexuality, along with Africans' purported tendencies toward heterosexual promiscuity, gender violence, and lack of the kind of internalized moral restraints that supposedly inhibit the spread of HIV in other cultures. Another common thread is a tendency toward age discrepancy in sexual relationships (mostly older men with younger women, girls, or even female infants), and, compared to the West, a relative absence of romantic affection and a predominance of transactional relationships (sex in exchange for money or gifts)...Rushton... claims a relationship between Africans' penis size and sexual behavior that can account for the high rates of HIV/AIDS among women in Africa and in the African diaspora.[16]

Epprecht's historical analysis reminds us that the representation of the AIDS pandemic in sub-Saharan Africa as *heterosexual* was consistent with the original, overall construction of HIV risk within the queer paradigm.[17] As with gay men, sex workers, and users of illicit drugs, "heterosexual transmission" was also assumed to be of queer and racialized forms. Rather than challenging the construction of HIV infection as a consequence of deviance, so-called heterosexuals found to be infected with HIV have always been described as having some mark of perversion: they were black or poor or had sometime in their past played around with anal intercourse. In the earliest discourses on AIDS as a global pandemic, the presumed heterosexuality of the African pandemic was said to mark its *difference* from the so-called Western epidemics that appeared to be concentrated among gay men, drug users, and the urban poor.[18] But the "heterosexuality" of the sub-Saharan African pandemic was not initially a competing paradigm to the reduction of disease to sexual and drug deviance as articulated within the queer paradigm. As Epprecht's account above demonstrates, all of the tropes of black sexual monstrosity and licentiousness, including the myth of the big black penis, have entered into scientific and public policy discourse to explain the "African AIDS" pandemic. Black Africans were simply represented as another set of sexual deviants, but on a continental—or rather, racial—scale.

The question, then, is why exclusive heterosexuality continues to be asserted in politicized and scholarly discourses of the African pandemic even by those who mean to break with the racist reduction of the regional pandemic to the outcome of "African sexuality." After all, O'Manique, Stillwaggon, and others are less interested in an anthropology of African sexuality than in using the presumed heterosexuality of the regional pandemic to launch forms of analysis that contextualize HIV risk within structural arrangements. Epprecht's careful deconstruction of the bad science involved in constructing "African heterosexuality" is undeniably useful and important, but that heterosexuality is a false category in AIDS epidemiology and discourse has never been that difficult to demonstrate, even if it has bewitched quite sophisticated scholars of the global pandemic.[19] That it has and continues to do so, however, suggests that "heterosexuality" plays an important discursive function in knowledges concerned with the AIDS pandemic in sub-Saharan Africa and beyond it to the degree that "African AIDS" is being reconstructed as exemplary of the global pandemic per se. Rather than argue over the proper definition of heterosexuality or even over the adequacy of exclusive heterosexuality as a descriptor for incidents of transmission and risk, then, I am interested in attending to the ideological work that this category performs for these scholars and its consequences.

The lure and function of heterosexuality in the emerging critical science on AIDS emerges from the structural logic of the queer paradigm. As discussed in chapter 1, Patton's queer paradigm denotes the ways in which HIV risk is constructed in professional, political, and public discourses as risk accruing to all of those marked as nonnormatively sexual or "queer." Notably, the article in which Patton introduced this concept is a critical reading of the early panic around the appearance of "heterosexual AIDS" in the United States. In the mid-1980s, as the official epidemiological profile of those found to be suffering AIDS continued to diversify, threatening the coherence of the ghettoizing impulse in AIDS discourses, Patton analyzed the explosive concern generated by a small number of AIDS cases—"an astonishing 59 (out of a U.S. total of nearly 8000)"—attributed to "heterosexual" transmission.[20] Whereas the prior four years had seen little concern in the nation's press or from its public officials, the appearance of heterosexuals among those with AIDS transformed the plague devastating the nation's inner-cities into what the Boston *Globe* was now calling a "national health emergency unprecedented in modern times" requiring "a unified federal battle plan."[21] Beyond the blatant hatred that determined who the nation bothered to care about, Patton detected two ideological impulses in this newly-acquired concern. First, what counted as heterosexuality was extremely restricted and normative. She writes:

> But the really interesting aspect of the heterosexual AIDS panic is the racism, sexism, and homophobia latent in the research and societal reaction.
>
> For starters, "heterosexual" in this case applies to "normal" people outside of the risk categories, give or take a few prostitutes. The heterosexual Haitians and IV-drug users (who some researcher want to reconsider as possible candidates for sexual transmission) are not counted as heterosexuals here. After all, they are drug addicts, and Black and, thus, not real, true heterosexuals who are white and live in nuclear families.[22]

Heterosexuality was (as it continues to be) much more connotative and normative than it is simply descriptive. It described particular kinds of racial, gendered, classed, and domesticated sexual relationships (white, non-drug-using, suburban, and nontransactional), rather than any and all sexual relationships between men and women.

What was panicky about heterosexual AIDS, then, was not that it was new—there had always been technically heterosexual people in AIDS counts—but that it seemed to be affecting *true heterosexuals*, and thus throwing into panic the dominant construction of risk. Immediately, therefore, researchers began looking for signs of queerness. Patton writes, "Researchers are...quick to note that almost all of the 59 supposed cases of heterosexual transmission were promiscuous, engaged in (yuck!) anal sex, or 'visited' prostitutes." She continues:

> A striking conclusion is drawn from the heterosexual cases: rather than challenging the idea that AIDS is a "gay disease," the cases confirm the idea that AIDS is related to deviant sex...The most striking evidence appears in the double talk about this new category of "heterosexuals," promiscuous and anally inclined though they may be. Much like the myth of predatory gays and lesbians or dark-skinned people with irresistible sexual charms, the underlying message is that heterosexuals don't normally do these things unless they are exposed to these exotic sexual elements.[23]

Heterosexuality was, therefore, both the *other* of so-called HIV risk groups as well as that which was *at risk* and in need of protection from contaminating exposure to "exotic sexual elements." Immunitary logic was at full alert: heterosexuality was in danger of being infected by the deviant and dangerous practices of perverts, practices like anal sex, promiscuity, and visits to prostitutes, all of which were supposed to lead to AIDS.[24]

As Patton demonstrates, then, the figure of *true heterosexuality* has outlined and exposed the queer paradigm's insistence that HIV risk is determined by deviant behaviors. True heterosexuality is the fantasy norm around which risk/deviance is distributed, which has made it a necessary discursive category from the very beginnings of the known epidemic. This is why Patton has insisted throughout her writing on the AIDS epidemic that heterosexuals, including heterosexual women, have been represented in AIDS knowledge from the very beginning. The problem is that they have been represented within the phobic logic of the queer paradigm as its constitutive "other."[25]

Thus, it was within the frame of the queer paradigm that *true heterosexuality* in all of its normative splendor appeared as a potential line of attack on the behavioralist and volunteerist logics of dominant HIV risk knowledges, but only on the condition that it distinguish itself from "deviant behaviors." Indeed, this is the discursive force of the assertion of heterosexuality in critical scholarship on the AIDS pandemic, especially scholarship focused on the pandemic in sub-Saharan Africa. It is meant to ward off the charge of queerness, with Africans represented not as sexual deviants but as normal, or at least relatively normal, heterosexuals. Evidence of broad heterosexual transmission has thus been offered as an exit from the claustrophobia of the queer paradigm, with its myopic and salacious fantasies of individuals and their behaviors, out into an account of *context*, first in terms of how transmission is structured (the social structuring of risk behaviors) and then in terms of the structuring of ecologies of disease. If HIV risk is not a mark of deviance, the critical scholars suggest, then it must be a mark of some other contextual issue. But in staging their critique of the queer paradigm from the position of its structural "other"— which is to say, in following the exit seemingly offered by the queer paradigm—scholars of the global pandemic have in fact left the queer paradigm intact, functioning alongside accounts of context and shaping the way that context is described. The assertion of dominant or exclusive heterosexual transmission has demonstrated, but also has participated in, the persistence of the queer paradigm, not its displacement.

Anthropologist Nancy Scheper-Hughes's somewhat notorious 1994 essay, "AIDS and the Social Body," represents an early salvo in the mobilization of heterosexuality against the queer paradigm.[26] In this essay, Scheper-Hughes called for breaking with the behavioral reductionism of dominant HIV risk discourses by "view[ing] AIDS from the perspective of those groups—but especially poor, heterosexual women who are not IV drug users or sex workers—often left out of AIDS discourse and prevention programs"[27] when considering the emerging epidemics of South and Central America and the Caribbean. Scheper-Hughes introduces this division in the service of her argument that poor, heterosexual women are not sovereign agents of their sexuality like the abstract subjects of dominant AIDS-prevention discourses, but must negotiate their sexuality with male partners in relation to whom they are handicapped by structured gender inequality. This fact, also made by other feminist critics of the dominant and global AIDS-prevention imaginary, exposes its inherent masculinism and individualism, both in representations of sexuality and in strategies of risk reduction. "AIDS educational programs," she writes, "assume that women, like gay and heterosexual men, are able to negotiate safe sex and that all they need is clear and specific information."[28] But the distinction that she stages in this essay between "poor, heterosexual women" and "IV drug users or sex workers" is neither epidemiologically nor theoretically necessary. There is, first, no reason to believe that these *kinds* of women are easily separable in actual social life.[29] Rich troves of historical research and ethnographic evidence exist calling into question the representation of both "sex workers" and "IV drug users" as distinct, separate forms of personhood, especially outside Euro-American industrialized countries but even within them. While the scholarship critiquing "prostitution" is more well-known, one of the lessons of ethnographic research on drug use has been that injecting users very often do not match the stereotype of the out-of-control addict.[30] They may have relatively stable housing, relationships, and employment. This, of course, is not always true, and may be less true of those who have suffered HIV infection, but it is true enough to call into question both descriptions of and prevention efforts for drug users. Sociologically and historically, however, the relative stability of many users of illicit substances demonstrates that specific social conditions are necessary to turn drug use into social and personal pathology. We return again to the conceptual distinction between acts and identities, and the impossibility of containing acts within identities. Neither drug use nor sex work are necessarily associated with clearly identified kinds of people, kinds who can be easily separated from others. Tellingly, this initial staging distinction quickly breaks down even within Scheper-Hughes's essay as her ethnographic observations on the emerging AIDS epidemic in Brazil turn to street children and transvestites who, like poor women, are socially disempowered in sexual life and often turn to irregular or full-time prostitution to support themselves.[31] She is unable to hold the distinction, in part because it is false in social life.

The discursive work of the distinction, however, is not undone by the sociological facts. Scheper-Hughes's essay stages a critique of the individualism and masculinism of biomedical individualism not by demonstrating its inadequacy relative to those whom it targets (and therefore calling into question the entire dramatics of the queer paradigm) but by asserting its inadequacy for "poor, heterosexual women" who are not sovereign subjects of their behaviors. In so doing, the presumption of adequacy is allowed to continue to adhere to those other (queer) subjects, the ones who "behave" in ways that put them at risk and who might be served by knowledge-based, behavioral programs. And indeed, Scheper-Hughes, like many other scholars, justifies this sleight of hand by invoking the story that US gay men "in such receptive and enlightened places as San Francisco" were able to significantly transform their AIDS epidemic through behavior modification.[32] This story seems to verify the truth of behavioral reductionism in the instance of first-world gay men. But there has only ever been problematic and contradictory evidence for the truth of this story, none of which has been entirely able to account for the ongoing epidemic among US gay men and its race and class contours. The discursive function of this story, however, has been to imply that "behaviors" as a category of analysis may be adequate or true for gay men—and by extension, other "queers" like IV drug users and sex workers—in ways that it is not for "poor heterosexuals," especially women. The story of gay men's success, no matter its actual truth value, has functioned more often than not as an opportunity for withdrawing scholarly and political concern from gay men and their continued suffering in the AIDS epidemic, notably with a transformed race and class profile.[33]

The ultimately phobic distinction between heterosexuals and queers has only deepened to the degree that heterosexuality has been further *naturalized* in the emerging ecological scholarship on poverty as the context for embodied vulnerability to HIV. For Scheper-Hughes as with scholars ranging from Paul Farmer to Colleen O'Manique, the problem of HIV risk inheres in the social relationships indexed by modes of transmission. In this way, they continue to problematize AIDS in terms of transmission practices, even as they socialize those practices. Thus for Scheper-Hughes, poor heterosexual women's HIV risk is posed in terms of the question of "sexual citizenship," a concept she introduces to theorize the gendered, political and economic conditions that shape women's experiences of and decision-making (in)capacities in relation to their sexuality.[34] At its worst (and all too often), this line of reasoning has led to the kind of flat-footed analysis that Alison Katz has called "gender diversions": racist depictions of ultra-patriarchal Third World men sexually abusing passive Third World women. Writing against these gender diversions, she asks,

> How can it possibly have escaped the notice of these researchers that men in sub Saharan Africa are about 250 times more vulnerable and oppressed than European, US American or Australian women in this and almost all other respects? Gender inequality is embedded in the real root causes of high rates of HIV prevalence which are desperate and incomparable poverty and powerlessness of people of both sexes in many poor countries. If such an *apolitical* gender debate has resulted in shifting the blame from all African people to *all African men*, it has failed.[35]

But not all of the research problematizing transmission behaviors has been so flat-footed. Much more important analyses have focused attention on the ways that transmission activities are socially structured in complex environments of economic necessity, social-institutional organization, cultural constraint, and competing desires, rather than through individual decision-making.[36]

The emergent scholarship on ecologies of health and their embodiment as increased disease susceptibility leverages heterosexuality against the queer paradigm in a slightly different way. Rather than heterosexuality, especially for women, serving as an analytic to socialize the account of HIV transmission—treating transmission as an index of social inequalities and vulnerability rather than individualistic "behaviors"—heterosexuality is *naturalized* in order to get to an *ecology of poverty*. For ecology of poverty scholars like Stillwaggon and Katz, the importance of poverty and embodied vulnerability is described as being indicated by the predominance of heterosexual transmission and the relative gender equality in HIV prevalence rates. These scholars then demonstrate that the social organization and practices of heterosexuality do not differ significantly or significantly enough between regions to account for their profound HIV rate differences.[37] At this point, heterosexuality is excused from the category of "behaviors" and becomes a natural form of human interaction that becomes a scene of disease transmission under certain conditions that are not intrinsic to it. "Breathing and having unprotected, penetrative vaginal sex" writes Alison Katz, "...are perhaps not quite in the same category but both can reasonably be seen as everyday human behaviors."[38] In order to depart from the phobic and victim-blaming discourse of queer behaviors, then, heterosexuality must be *naturalized* (and therefore discursively *neutralized*) in order to get to the ecological conditions under which HIV is able to emerge in epidemic proportions.

Relations of foreground and background are reversed. Under the queer paradigm, forms of heterosexuality are foregrounded as deviant practices lending themselves to risk of HIV transmission, while difference in the ecologies of human immiseration or human flourishing are fundamentally background issues. Better and worse analyses depend on the degree to which, and manner in which, these background conditions are described as structuring potential transmission practices (the foreground). Psychological or culturalist narratives of HIV risk practice, while the dominant public-health narratives, are politically and theoretically much worse than research that attempts to think about transmission risk practices within political economies of poverty, legality, racism, and gender.[39] (Indeed, had the latter research ever achieved dominance in epidemiological analysis or public-health practice, it might have achieved many of the same goals as an ecosocial model of disease, even without the deeper understanding of human physiology found in the ecosocial model.) The ecology of disease scholarship, in turn, pulls the queer paradigm's background—the ecologies of immiseration or flourishing—into the analytic foreground, and pushes heterosexual practice into the background. Heterosexuality recedes as simply the banal fact of human contact through which a virus may travel, but only if the conditions for its emergence as a mass and reproducible phenomenon are met: ecologies of human misery and embodied vulnerability. These ecologies are what matter.

Abstractly, this is all correct. Ecologies of disease emergence are the essential issue, and transmission routes are simply the by and large banal facts of human contact and sociability. Even injection drug use—the "behavior" seemingly furthest from "natural human needs"—is socially constructed to be risky only within certain environments of legal, social, and economic constraint, all of which could be reformed.[40] What is notable, however, is that no ecology of poverty scholar says this. Instead, the banality of human contact—its naturalness—has been reserved only for heterosexuality and reproduction (vertical transmission between mother and child) rather than being extended to all of the means through which HIV is transmitted among people.

Eileen Stillwaggon's *AIDS and the Ecology of Poverty* is arguably the most rigorous deconstruction of the behavioral reductionism of the queer paradigm and argument for the embodiment of extreme poverty as the basis for the pandemic in sub-Saharan Africa; so it is useful to track her analysis. As with other scholars, she launches her analysis by asserting heterosexual transmission as evidence for the priority of ecological conditions. As she writes, her "book is primarily about the heterosexual and vertical [mother to child] epidemics of HIV/AIDS. It is in those epidemics that the greatest difference in rate of infection between rich and poor countries occurs."[41] This difference, however, turns out not to be a matter of quantity but of type: heterosexual and vertical transmission are not simply greater in poorer countries, they describe different kinds of epidemics. The difference in type emerges clearly in Stillwaggon's text as she attempts to extend her analysis of the conditions of poverty that she argues have fueled the African AIDS pandemic to emerging epidemics in Latin America and the Caribbean. While both of the latter regions have epidemics with significant heterosexual transmission, their epidemics are also significantly attached to sexuality between men and drug use as modes of HIV transmission. Although in a succeeding chapter Stillwaggon masterfully contextualizes the drug-use-fueled AIDS epidemics in post-Soviet nations in terms of the mass impoverishment and social dislocation produced by the imposition of capitalism onto formerly socialist societies in the 1990s,[42] in the context of Latin America and the Caribbean, homosexuality and drug use are described as fundamentally Western and rich, connoting tropes of "Western decadence." Notice the way that "rich" and "poor" are mapping differences in kind in the following introductory comments to her chapter on the Latin American and Caribbean AIDS epidemics:

> Latin America represents a composite of the industrial and developing worlds, both in its economic performance and in its HIV epidemics...Most Latin American and Caribbean countries are ranked as middle-income and of medium human development. That ranking does not represent an intermediate stage between the developing and industrialized countries, however. Instead, it is the result of averaging the affluence of Latin America's modern sector and the extreme poverty and economic and political instability on which it uneasily rests. Latin America has the most unequal distribution of income of any world region, a fact that influences every aspect of its society and economy...Diseases of the poor (infectious and parasitic diseases) continue to claim a large percentage of lives, while the so-called diseases of affluence (chronic and degenerative diseases) contribute increasingly to morbidity and mortality, at higher age-adjusted rates among the poor than among the rich.
>
> Latin America and the Caribbean also have a dual HIV profile. The region mirrors the industrialized world in HIV epidemics among men who have sex with men and people who share needles, and it has a rapidly spreading heterosexual epidemic, as is the case in Sub-Saharan Africa and South Asia.[43]

Rather than understanding disease vulnerability among men who have sex with men and intravenous drug users as also conditioned by the wealth inequality of Latin American and Caribbean countries that Stillwaggon rightly notes as being fundamental to HIV transmission between men and women, she rhetorically equates the former modes of transmission with "diseases of affluence." HIV transmission sexually between men or through needle sharing is Western/rich/industrial while heterosexual transmission is Third World and poor. These two epidemiological profiles are not to be thought together, but independently as a "composite" of essentially different epidemics without a common base.

My effort here is not to accuse these authors of personal homophobia or to undermine their important sociological and epidemiological contributions to our understanding of the global AIDS pandemic. In fact, I find Stillwaggon to be one of the best scholars of the global pandemic. What I am trying to get at, however, is a theoretical and discursive structure that she shares with other scholars of AIDS that I find ultimately inadequate in its understanding of the dynamics of embodied vulnerability to HIV, if also fundamentally sexually conservative. My argument is that the category of "heterosexuality" actually restricts the broader critique opened up by an ecological understanding of disease vulnerability and HIV transmission. By resting the case for contextualizing factors on the fact of heterosexuality, the analytical and epidemiological direction opened up by an understanding of the embodiment of social ecology has functioned in a *supplementary* relation to the behavioral account of HIV transmission and disparities, rather than *displacing* it. The queer paradigm of behaviors has been allowed to continue functioning "in other places," primarily those marked as Western, homosexual, and masculine; often also in the context of HIV transmission through illicit drug use.[44] These "other places," however, also function reciprocally as a supplement to the account of heterosexuality, as a pressure valve for that category and the way that it seems to contain and pacify all instances of sexualized contact between social agents marked as men and those marked as women, from domestic intimacy to marital rape, from casual nonmonogamy to formal prostitution, from gendered inequality within courtship to organized mass rape in the context of regional wars. All of these relations seem to *count* as heterosexuality.

Collapsing different contexts of viral transmission under the bland figure of heterosexuality functionally restricts an accounting of violence as constitutive of the ecologies of AIDS, including the ecologies of violence in which men are infected with HIV. Rather, these ecologies are pacified as *poverty* in a static sense: poverty as a habitus or suffusing environment. The supplementary relationship that has been established between heterosexual and nonheterosexual transmission divides accounts of AIDS epidemic between ecologies of poverty that are embodied as increased susceptibility to HIV and the most traditional, pathologizing descriptions of risk behaviors: male homosexuality, prostitution, and injecting drug use. But in doing so, structured relations of social violence become invisible, with the exception of gender inequality. Indeed, much like the salacious descriptions of racialized and queer sexualities, reductive accounts of gender inequality—the "gender diversion" diagnosed by Katz—have become a way to avoid talking about structured forms of violence. Gender inequality's constraint on women's sexual and personal agency is very much a part of their vulnerability to HIV infection, but in the context of AIDS epidemic this constrained domestic agency is but a link in the chain of social relations that tie women and men to HIV in an organized manner.

If we are to understand the sub-Saharan pandemic and the racial structuring of the global pandemic—including for African and African diasporic women—accounts of ecologies of disease and vulnerability will need to move past the analytics of poverty and gender inequality encouraged by recourse to the fantasy of normative, heterosexual transmission, and toward understandings of the specific ways that global black populations are subject to racialized forms of domination and abandonment. This is not to deny the importance of poverty, inequality, or gender, but to insist that these analitics must be radicalized by attention to the force of antiblack racism. This is the fundamental lesson of Black feminism.[45] Like the US epidemic, the pandemic in sub-Saharan Africa—including but not restricted to the South African epidemic—has been organized by racialized exclusion—both economic and social—and structured forms of domination and violence, but AIDS scholars have been entirely resistant to attending to the force of antiblack racism beyond denouncing the racist representations of Africans and their sexualities. AIDS scholars seem to have no tools for connecting racist representations to material economies of accumulation, dispossession, and violence. Unable to connect racist representations to social force, AIDS scholars analogize racial formation in other terms, especially class and gender.[46] Thus, we arrive at poverty, inequality, and gender, rather than at structured antiblack racism. But racist representation should be understood as an index of racist structural formation: antiblack animus, as seen in the representations of exotic and violent black sexualities, emerges from and materializes within global flows of power.

The black American experience with AIDS suggests two avenues for thinking beyond the critique of representations to understand the color of suffering in the global pandemic. The US epidemic that I have described emerged from and is sustained by the convergence of phobic, antiblack exclusion and phobic, antiblack domination, each mobilized by and articulated through the US state. Concretely, this took form through economic and social reorganization around and away from urban blacks, reconsolidating the "dark ghettos" as the *other* of national economic integration, and through state domination via hyper incarceration. For global racial formations, "the state" is more firmly articulated within the structures and discourse of globalization, with international and transnational institutions playing a more direct role in the organization and execution of technologies of domination, exploitation, and abandonment. And yet, the global racial calculus remains remarkably uniform, even if racial discourses differ, and the universal derogation of blackness is materialized as uniquely black suffering. Structured exclusion and structured domination, especially as they overlap, also organize the experience of vulnerability for black peoples of sub-Saharan Africa and the broader African diaspora.

What follows does not presume to *explain* the AIDS pandemic in sub-Saharan Africa but to open up potential lines of inquiry repressed by the current accounts of heterosexual transmission and ecologies of poverty. Drawing upon existing scholarship, I suggest that rather than the conditions of impoverishment or the conditions of everyday sexuality, accounts of the African pandemic attend to the racial structuring of violence: from the cold-blooded violence of World Bank technocratic decision-making about the ordering of capitalist domination to the emergence and persistence of the postcolonial wars. The question then becomes how the ecologies of poverty and gendered heterosexuality connect to and are ordered by these structures of violence, without reducing or displacing the centrality of those structures.

Globalization, or Not

To begin to understand the unique suffering of sub-Saharan Africa demands, first, a more precise reading of its place in—or rather, its exclusion from—capitalist globalization. Prevailing discourses on globalization emphasize increased integration of economies and cultures on a global scale, if altogether unevenly. Increasingly, the state as a unit of integration for societies, cultures, and economies is said to be superseded by forces of integration, especially economic, that function on a global scale, with new relations of inequality and difference. AIDS, in turn, has often been hailed as the "first epidemic of globalization," and routinely represented as resting upon the global infrastructure of inte-grated communications (especially market integration), the new identities and differences (especially around sexuality), and redis-tributed or reinforced relations of inequality, not only between societies but within them.[47] In response, materialist scholars of the pandemic have argued for attending less to the new modes of globalized capital integration, transportation, and identity than to the underside of globalization: the simultaneous intensifica-tion of economic inequality—including the resulting economic and political migrations—along with the weakening of the state's role as protector of population health. The problem with global-ization is less its reorganization of sexual identities and sexual linkages than with its intensification of poverty and inequality, including through the destruction of basic ameliorative institu-tions like public health.[48] The AIDS pandemic travels through these ecologies of poverty and inequality. For instance, in her investigation of the role of global economic and political struc-turing on AIDS in Uganda and broader sub-Saharan African, Colleen O'Manique literally titles it "globalization's pandemic."

The description of globalization as "uneven integration," how-ever, has a kind of flattening effect, with scholars routinely fall-ing back onto a dichotomous distinction between "rich and poor countries," including recourse to a generalized "Third World." In this discourse, sub-Saharan Africa is treated as another, if extreme, instance of poor countries of the Third World, as seen in the routine expectation of an "Africanized" epidemic in other poor regions and countries, like India and China.[49] What allows India or China to be "like Africa" is their common mass poverty. But as Neil Smith has argued, "Since the 1970s, the Third World has been restructured out of existence."[50] Smith argues that while a number of the countries and regions that constituted the Third World under the regime of modernization instituted through Cold War policies emanating from both the West and the Soviet block have been integrated or partially integrated into the post-Cold War globalizing capitalism, sub-Saharan Africa is unique as a region in its "virtual systematic expulsion from capitalism."[51] He writes:

> But this attraction of some underdeveloped economies to the global lodestone of capital has been matched since the 1980s by a virtual expulsion of other economies, far more dramatic than even under the aegis of modernization. This expulsion has gone virtually unremarked, even if the consequent unprecedented destruction of everyday life has been fitfully recorded. From the Sahel famine of 1968–1974 to the Central African genocide that started in Rwanda (and to a lesser extent Burundi) in 1994 and spread to Zaire by 1997, Sub-Saharan Africa has borne the brunt of what we as academics politely refer to as globalization or global restructuring.[52]

Smith's analysis challenges the description of sub-Saharan Africa as an instance of poor countries or part of a larger Third World. Rather than being even unequally integrated into globalization, sub-Saharan Africa has been expelled from it. We need not romanticize global economic integration to attend to the difference between exploitation and exclusion even from exploitation.

Smith describes sub-Saharan Africa's exclusion from the global economy in racial terms borrowed heavily from the North American experience. He calls sub-Saharan Africa the world's "black ghetto" and describes its relationship to capital markets as one of "redlining," in both instances suggesting an analogy with the US black experience. Indeed, as Black Studies scholar Jared Sexton has argued, globalization may best be understood "as uneven economic, political, and cultural integration along the East-West axis" that not just excludes, but constitutes itself against sub-Saharan Africa, and global black populations, broadly, in the form of a "global apartheid."[53] Global integration is being structured as nonblack integration, if unequal and uneven. He suggests, in turn, that the "political economy and cultural politics of the AIDS pandemic—the grammar and geography of the greatest public-health crisis in recorded history— have only solidified these tendencies."[54]

These analyses call attention to the specific racial structuring of sub-Saharan Africa's relation to globalization. Rather than a poor region among other poor regions in an increasingly globalized capitalism, sub-Saharan Africa is better understood as excluded or expelled from globalization. This expulsion, in turn, has a specifically antiblack impetus that is irreducible to capitalist logic. *Inequality* fails to capture what is unique about sub-Saharan Africa on a global scale and the ways that this condition pertains, or not, to other places. sub-Saharan Africa is not properly "poor," as opposed to "rich," or unequal within the integrated global economy; it has been virtually excluded from globalization. Exclusion—or more precisely, "disinvestment and abandonment"[55]—rather than inequality per se, better explains the structuring conditions for the pandemic in sub-Saharan Africa, and what distinguishes it from places like China or India to which it is often compared, at least at the scale of the nation or region.

What makes sub-Saharan Africa exemplary, then, is its geographic and demographic size as a zone of black exclusion and abandonment. For exclusion and abandonment also describe many of the zones most affected by the global pandemic, from the US black ghettos described in chapter 2 to Brazilian favelas and most of the black Caribbean.[56] For the greater Atlantic, the world most clearly marked by what Saidiya Hartman has called the "afterlife of slavery,"[57] these zones of exclusion and abandonment are not only primarily racially black, they are paradigmatically so. Which is to say, these are zones constituted through the force of antiblack racism. A proper accounting of the place of sub-Saharan Africa in terms of "the globe" calls attention to the structuring role of antiblack racism in the forming of ecologies of vulnerability to HIV on a global scale. The global pandemic is, of course, not contained within black populations, but antiblack exclusion and abandonment have structured its emergence and dispersion. Other regions of the world, both in part and in whole, fear "Africanization" not only of their economies[58] but of their epidemics, demonstrating the paradigmatic blackness of exclusion and abandonment, and of their effects.

From Heterosexuality to Structures of Violence

Scholarly and political reversion to heterosexual transmission as a defining feature of the African pandemic has not only articulated a misleading flattening of differences within the figure of "the poor,"[59] it has also blocked attention to the ways that embodied vulnerability and relationships of exposure in sub-Saharan Africa have been organized by concrete forms of violence and domination. This blockage appears in discourse and scholarship as a trend or emphasis more than a definitive exclusion, but the pacification of the ecologies of disease that I tracked above tends to sideline or exclude longstanding scholarship connecting the formation of regional and local epidemics in sub-Saharan Africa to organized domination and violence, along with nonsexual modes of transmission. Again, I make no pretension to an exhaustive survey here, which would require systematically recovering and developing further a large body of scattered anthropological, historical, and epidemiological scholarship: a project that is beyond this one. But three broad institutional arrangements appear to have been essential to the emergence and structuring of the regional pandemic in sub-Saharan Africa far beyond domestic gendered heterosexuality: labor, war, and medicine. Or rather, these three institutional arrangements have articulated sex between men and women into larger formations of concentrated exposure and vulnerability to HIV.

The Structure of Labor

Certain forms of *organized labor exploitation*, particularly mining, have long been known to structure not only the South African epidemic but the broader regional pandemic. The organization of mining labor functions in a manner analogous to mass incarceration examined in chapter 3. Mine labor in southern Africa has been structured to be antifamilial.[60] Men who work in the mines live in camps near the mine during the periods that they are in it, returning to wives and families who tend to live in villages at some distance from the mine. The labor organization of mines therefore creates a continuous mechanism of concentration and dispersal, as men concentrate at the mine and then return. Near the mining camps, as with other places where single or singled men work, like military bases, women set up small businesses to provide services, from cooking and cleaning to sex. The miners also set up social and sexual relations in and near the mine camps, not only among themselves but with the women working nearby. Thus, multiple networks of sexuality, exchange, and affection overlap in and spread out from the mining camps, networks that do not easily settle into categories like heterosexual, homosexual, familial, monetary, monogamous, or polygamous. My point, however, is not to "straighten out" these relationships but to attend to the way that these overlapping networks are created by a structure of economic domination that also concentrates both embodied vulnerability and conditions of exposure to HIV.

It makes little sense to describe the male mine workers and the women who sell services and also sometimes sex to them as "risk-takers" with the miners' wives and families passively "at risk."[61] Rather, mine workers, the women of the mine camps, and village families are together articulated into a political-economic and racial structure of exploitation that creates conditions of intensified bodily danger and vulnerability, which in turn is also a social organization that intensifies exposure to HIV and then disperses it. All of these people have been put at risk in differentiated ways that are articulated within a structure of domination. Indeed, mine labor, like other forms of health-destroying, de-familial, semi-migratory, mass labor has been a near-perfect social technology for epidemic dispersion of HIV.

Warfare

A number of scholars have also pointed to the place of *war* in the emergence and dispersion of epidemic HIV in sub-Saharan Africa. War is an engine for disease, and this has been no less true for HIV.[62] As Nana Poku reminds us, "in the absence of penicillin, the war-ravaged Europe of the late 1940s would have been devastated by epidemics of syphilis and gonorrhea."[63] In turn, major centers of the regional AIDS pandemic in sub-Saharan Africa have been war-torn environments, including civil war-torn Uganda,[64] apartheid South Africa, and the nations surrounding South Africa that were subject to its policy of political disruption. Indeed, as Mariella Baldo and Antonio Jorge Cabral argue,

[T]he most important historical structural process concerning HIV transmission in Southern Africa are the LIW [low-intensity wars] and the disruption of the economy, particularly the rural economy. Various population groups are forced into continuous movements, including displacement flight from the war affected areas, regular armies and groups of bandits, rural populations moving to towns (joining the poverty and marginality circle including prostitution and street children), and rural populations moving near barracks for trading (promiscuity).[65]

These observations join other scholarship connecting AIDS epidemic to the processes and effects of warfare. For instance, based upon women's self-reporting, feminist medical anthropologist Brooke Grundfest Schoepf has long argued that women's increased vulnerability to HIV in sub-Saharan Africa included the prevalence of rape within contexts of warfare, including but not limited to the use of mass rape as a tool of terror.[66] Increased sexual violence, however, takes place within a broader social and biological context especially suited to infectious disease.

Protracted warfare increases embodied vulnerability to disease and exposure to HIV. At the most fundamental level, warfare destroys or seriously disrupts the infrastructure necessary for human persistence and thriving. Towns and cities are destroyed, as are food crops and animals, leaving people without shelter, food and water, or other means of subsistence. Large populations of people are set adrift, housed in temporary refugee sheltering (if at all) that is often lacking in basic human infrastructure like adequate, clean water or adequate sanitation. World Health Organization communicable disease officials Máire Connolly and David Heymann report that "mortality rates over 60 times higher than baseline rates have been recorded [in refugee camps] after such displacement."[67] Under these situations, women and children are made additionally vulnerable to forms of sexual commerce or sexual assault that may expose them to HIV by soldiers, mercenaries, or other marauders who prey upon the displaced, or by men within the refugee camps where cultural systems of social and sexual regulation have broken down. War, therefore, may be understood as a complex social mechanism that destroys ecologies of health, leading to greater embodied susceptibility to disease; that increases exposure to HIV through forms of sexual and other violence, including the use of rape as a tool of terror on the part of competing armies; and that organizes the mass dispersion of disease through forced migration, refugee settlement, and return policies, as well as through troop movements. Indeed, as has been demonstrated by the histories of other infectious diseases and also within the history of the global AIDS pandemic, warfare organizes the "perfect storm" for disease emergence and dispersion.

Medical Transmission

Finally, there is persistent and longstanding evidence that *medical transmission* of HIV has been important, and possibly fundamental, to the AIDS pandemic in sub-Saharan Africa, as it has been in many other places.[68] As Eileen Stillwaggon remarks, "There is plentiful evidence in scientific studies to support the observations of those who work in poor countries that medical and quasi-medical HIV transmission accounts for at least a significant minority of infections in Africa, Asia, and Latin America."[69] Different scholars suggest different degrees to which medical transmission has played a part in overall epidemics in the region, from very little to extensive. While Edward Hooper, in his *The River,* has argued that the African regional pandemic emerged not from sexual transmission at all but from contaminated polio vaccine administered to colonial subjects in the 1950s,[70] a variety of other scholars have long suggested that too little attention has been dedicated to investigating the role of poorly regulated and financed biomedical distributions systems, including the global trade in blood products, given their wide use as reparative therapy for anemia in sub-Saharan Africa prior to the official advent of the pandemic.[71] While there is less reason to suspect that medical transmission is solely responsible for the *replication* of the regional pandemic in the present, these scholars suggest that it might have been essential to its *emergence* as a pandemic per se, and sufficient evidence is available for treating it as one, among other important engines in the reproduction of that pandemic over time.

Conclusion

It may very well be that transmission between men and women has become the predominant form of HIV transmission in sub-Saharan Africa, and scholars have to my mind demonstrated conclusively that impoverishment has been essential to the widespread embodiment of vulnerability that has enabled the reproduction and expansion of the pandemic. Discursively, however, the *hetero-sexuality-poverty nexus* has trained scholarly and political attention in ways that tend toward the description of poverty as a relatively static and suffusing environment or condition rather than the resultant of structured relations of domination and violence that have themselves organized bodily vulnerability and incidents of exposure to HIV. The black health tradition challenges us, however, to look directly at those structured relations as the fundamental cause of the AIDS pandemic in sub-Saharan Africa, just as an analogous, antiblack racial formation has organized both vulnerability and exposure to HIV for black Americans. Indeed, to again paraphrase Marxist health scholar Evan Stark, any account of the AIDS pandemic in sub-Saharan Africa is at best incomplete, and at worst wrong, to the degree that it fails to attend to the structured relations of domination and violence—both political-economic and antiblack—that have not simply created broad conditions of embodied ill health and vulnerability, but that have created concrete structures of vulnerability, exposure, and concern.[72]

Conclusion

The Politics of Crisis

In her effort to de-(melo)dramatize scenes of everyday or ongoing precarity and pull the narratives of social suffering away from the trope of "trauma," Lauren Berlant defines the experience of *slow death* as "the physical wearing out of a population in a way that points to its deterioration as defining conditions of its experience and historical existence."[1] She refers here to those zones or modes of existence that are structured through regimes of governmentality and capitalist domination, not for thriving or life-building, but for attrition, wearing out, and just getting by (or not). Slow death is less active or agential—less sovereign—than representations of genocide or war, and is more similar to my own effort to think about the relationship between the AIDS pandemic and the kinds of human ecologies that "*foster* life or *disallow* it to the point of death."[2] Slow death describes one of the ways that the power to *disallow* life "to the point of death" manifests itself.

Berlant argues that the trope of slow death takes form through a displacement in the concept of the event. Here, she follows Foucault in thinking through the narrative structure of *eventalization*. In a companion piece to her "Slow Death," Berlant writes, "When Foucault talks about eventalization, he refers to a need to move analytically beyond the moment when a happening moves into common sense, or a process congeals into an object-event that conceals its immanence, its potentially unfinished or enigmatic activity."[3] Eventalization therefore engages in a kind of covering over or crowding out of attention to that which is in process or unfinished; it frames a scene. Slow death, Berlant argues, is a condition of living that is not marked primarily through the temporal or spatial dimensions of the event, but rather through those of what she names "environment."[4] She writes, "Slow death prospers not in traumatic events, as discrete time-framed phenomena like military encounters and genocides can appear to do, but in temporally labile environments whose qualities and whose contours in time and space are often identified with the presentness of ordinariness itself."[5] Environment, as Berlant uses the term, is analytically similar to the concept of "ecology" that I have drawn from ecosocial epidemiology, where "structural conditions are suffused through a variety of mediations."[6] Environments may, of course, be marked by events, but the effectivity of an environment—including its effectivity in wearing out, attrition, slow death—does not take place through the rhythm of events. Rather, it takes place through a kind of ordinariness, routine, everydayness that overwhelms. In order to attend to the mode of power that structures zones of slow death, it is essential to attend to the distinction between event and environment, and it is especially important to resist pulling the deployment of slow death as environment into the temporal and spatial register of the event.

Berlant identifies "crisis" as a key discourse through which environment or ecology is pulled into the narrative trope of the event, or eventalized. She writes, "Often when scholars and activists apprehend the phenomenon of slow death in long-term conditions of privation, they choose to misrepresent the duration and scale of the situation by calling a *crisis* that which is a fact of life and has been a defining fact of life for a given population that lives that crisis in ordinary time."[7] The so-called obesity epidemic is her case study. This "epidemic" reveals both the lure and the danger of crisis rhetoric in transforming environment or ecology into event. "Obesity" is framed in public discourses as a scene of failed will and failed agency, when not agro-corporate murder. Inflated dramas of sovereign agency fill the scene, even and especially in their absence. But the rise of obesity as a broadly distributed health condition demands another mode of attention if one is to be marginally accountable to the relationship between the classes of those who suffer—the proletarian and subproletarian classes—and the conditions of attrition and wearing out that constitute the zone of living on of the obese. Obesity is deeply and complexly tied to precariousness, anxiety, and malnutrition, but crisis rhetoric tends to misrecognize this bad life of slow death as lives lived badly.

In order to approach the environment or ecology of obesity, Berlant calls for displacing the rhetoric of epidemic-as-event in favor of the figure of the *endemic*.[8] Again, the distinction is in ways of attending to phenomena, both theoretically and in terms of governmentality. Berlant pulls the distinction between epidemic and endemic from Foucault's genealogy of biopower in which he tracks the development in eighteenth-century governmental rationality, alongside the traditional concern with epidemic disease, of a concern with the *endemic*, conceived as those illnesses that are tied to the foundations of society and environment and therefore difficult to eradicate.[9] Whereas epidemic disease "swooped down on life" and caused widespread but still spatially and temporally contained death (in the order of the event), the endemic is a form of death that is "something permanent, something that slips into life, perpetually gnaws at it, diminishes it and weakens it."[10] Not even a series of events, the endemic is rather the perpetual gnawing on health or vitality, even to the point of death. "Slow death," Berlant declares, "occupies the temporalities of the endemic."[11]

As I close this book, I am trying to think about the urgency to *do something* and the ways in which it is enrolled into managing the AIDS epidemic, rather than transforming the conditions of its possibility. It is commonplace in AIDS discourse to begin discussions about controlling the pandemic by stating something like, "In the absence of vaccines and treatments the only way to combat AIDS is to prevent exposure to and transmission of HIV infection."[12] In other words, without what Allan Brandt has called the "magic bullet" of a biomedical cure,[13] all we have is the difficult and delicate arts of prevention, conceived as the disruption of incidences of exposure. This book stands opposed to the sentiment of this statement, not because of any hope in a biomedical miracle nor because of the important objection that treatment is also a form of prevention. Rather, I object to the commonplace that prevention is all that we (who?) can do to control the AIDS pandemic without a vaccine or cure for Human Immunodeficiency Virus (HIV). I know that I am not alone in finding the way that AIDS politics has been reduced to behavioral therapeutics and movements for drug-provision shocking. Most of the authors examined here also object to this myopia. We object to the ways that "prevention" is staged solely as intervention into scenes of exposure and transmission. The reduction of disease governance to "prevention" contains within it what Sylvia Noble Tesh has called "hidden arguments" about both the source of disease and the proper way to govern a society.[14] One of the functions of biomedical individualism as organized by the queer paradigm has been to privatize responsibility for disease risk. It fits handily with the broader neoliberal project.[15]

Much of what Berlant theorizes as slow death resonates with the account of the AIDS pandemic as I have been describing it, especially in the move toward the environmental or ecological in understanding health and disease, but I also want to attend closely to Berlant's warning against crisis discourse, moving toward an account of slow death as what she calls "crisis ordinariness." I want to attend to the ways that crisis rhetoric presents a constant impulse to distortion, from endemicity and slow death to scenes of inflated agency. The warning against crisis rhetoric is not new in the history of AIDS cultural criticism. For instance, Simon Watney, early in the epidemic, analyzed the way in which the construction of AIDS as a "moral panic" had been used to engage in the most repressive kinds of state action against people living with AIDS in the broadest sense, including but not limited to people living with HIV infection, from immigration restrictions against people infected with (or suspected of being infected with) HIV, to the censoring of safer sex and other forms of literature that dared to be pro-gay and pro-sex, to the criminalization of sex for people living with HIV.[16] Precisely by constructing the AIDS epidemic as a panic or crisis, statist forces on the right, the center, and the left have been able to circumvent liberal safeguards on civil liberties, let alone check the political aspirations of resistant social movements. There is nothing new in this history—crisis has a long history in liberal democracies as the rhetoric through which liberalism is suspended, or suspended for the socially disempowered—but that it is not new demonstrates yet again the danger that Berlant indexes with her warning against the use of crisis rhetoric on the part of activists and intellectuals.

Berlant's warning also points to a further way in which crisis has been built into AIDS discourse beyond its uses for repressive state action, including discourses that have emerged from resistant activists and scholars. As discussed in chapter 1, medical historian David McBride frames his history of the black health tradition by asking why that tradition has had so little sway in the understanding of and intervention into the US epidemic, particularly as experienced by black Americans. One way to describe his answer is the victory of "crisis" over "crisis ordinariness." McBride argues that one of the key material and discursive forces blocking the black health tradition has been the biomedical reduction of AIDS to HIV infection, abstracting it from the broader urban health crisis as suffered by black people. In Berlant's language, following Foucault, the *endemic* has been described as *epidemic*. The biomedical construction of AIDS—its "invention" in the precise sense analyzed by Cindy Patton[17]—automatically includes within it a crisis-oriented sense of temporality and mode of attention. To the degree that AIDS science and politics have ascribed to this biomedical reduction, they have misapprehended antiblack racial domination lived in the mode of slow death as lives lived poorly. At its most naïve, this misapprehension appears as the insipid insistence upon risk-reduction prevention strategies, generally behavioral, directed at people already living on the edge. We saw this, for instance, in chapter 2 in the Centers for Disease Control and Prevention (CDC) research on "Communities in Crisis," where even after identifying extreme urban poverty as the dominant indicator for risk of HIV infection, public health officials could offer little more than targeted prevention interventions.

As I see it, the long history of critical scholarship on the AIDS epidemic, the scholarship critical of the biomedical reductionism of viruses and behaviors stripped of context, has for its entire history been trying to find its way back to the black materialist tradition in health, understanding the epidemic as an expression of the social relations that structure ecologies of embodied vulnerability to disease. From Cindy Patton's critique of the reductionism of the queer paradigm, to Merrill Singer's description of the urban epidemic as actually *syndemic* with the greater inner-city health crisis, to Roderick Wallace's geographic analysis of HIV's dispersion through the structured zones of neoliberal abandonment and racial apartheid, scholars have been trying to move the analysis of AIDS from the *epidemic* back to the *endemic*. This has been the power and the virtue of the materialist tradition in the health sciences. With few exceptions, however, this history has been resistant to treating antiblack racial structuring as fundamental, leaving black disproportionality, even relative to other people of color, as a mystery. It is my hope that this book begins to demystify the extraordinary suffering of black people by understanding antiblack racism as central to the historical and social processes that have shaped the AIDS epidemic in the United States, and to the degree that the US experience is analogous, shaped the global pandemic as well.

To return to the black health tradition in our understanding of the US AIDS epidemic, however, is to take up the question of crisis again, but differently. The black health tradition is not simply a manner of knowing. It has been a wing of the broader project of black liberation, a response to the crisis of antiblackness itself. In relation to this crisis, health and liberation are inseparable. Alondra Nelson's recent book, *Body and Soul: The Black Panther Party and the Fight against Medical Discrimination*, a history of the health activism organized through the Black Panther Party in the 1960s and 1970s, may serve as a guide. As Nelson demonstrates, the Black Panther Party engaged in significant and systematic health activism during its brief flourishing, an activism that has only partially survived its historical defeat and retrenchment. But during its moment, the health activism of the Panthers posed and addressed the problems of ill health and disease for black people as consequences of antiblack racism and its effects, including lack of access to healthcare; unsafe housing, streets, water, and air; and malnutrition. The Panthers addressed this health crisis on at least three fronts: the immediate provision of health services; attention to the conditions structuring disease and ill health, like poverty-related malnutrition; and the broader liberatory project for which the Party is better known. As she writes, this "health rights activism of the 1960s and 1970s was an extension of the push for equal liberties and an effort to bridge the stubborn gap that separated civil and social citizenship."[18] The problem of *endemic* ill health was addressed through the politics of black liberation.

The black health tradition, broadly conceived as a part of the black liberatory tradition, suggests that while Berlant's attention to the lure of "crisis rhetoric" is essential, the alternative is not something other than crisis, but another crisis. What is to be distinguished is not crisis from something else, but a distinction within crisis itself. In his oft-quoted thesis on the philosophy of history, Walter Benjamin declares, "The tradition of the oppressed teaches us that the 'state of emergency' in which we live is not the exception but the rule. We must attain a conception of history that is in keeping with this insight. Then we shall realize that it is our task to bring about a real state of emergency."[19] The black health tradition—a tradition of the oppressed, if ever there was one—attends to the AIDS crisis not as an exception, but as the rule, as an expression of the "state of emergency" that is the rule, the everyday, the endemic. It is a mode of attention that attends to the endemic as crisis, in relation to which liberation is the answer. Given the absolute centrality of antiblack racism in structuring the conditions of emergence and mechanisms of dispersion of the AIDS epidemic—the endemic conditions in which the epidemic could emerge as such—for those of us truly interested in a critical politics of AIDS, the black liberatory tradition is the model for thinking about how to respond to the AIDS crisis. The proper politics for the AIDS crisis is the politics of liberation, liberation from the structured relation of oppression and exclusion that have been organized through antiblack racism. These *state intimacies* are the "risk practices" from which black people especially, but also all of us caught up in the suffering of the AIDS epidemic, must be liberated.

Notes

1 Rethinking AIDS in Black America

1. US population data from United States Census Bureau, *Income, poverty, and health insurance coverage in the United States: 2011*, Current Population Reports, P60–243 (Washington, DC: US Government Printing Office, 2012), accessed May 20, 2013, from http://www.census.gov/prod/2012pubs/p60–243.pdf. HIV pre-valence data drawn from CDC, "Prevalence of undiagnosed HIV infection among persons aged ≥13 years—National HIV surveillance system, United States, 2005–2008," *MMWR* 61, Suppl (June 15, 2012): 57–64. HIV incidence data drawn from CDC, "Estimated HIV incidence in the United States, 2007–2010," *HIV Surveillance Supplemental Report* 17, no. 4 (2012), accessed February 18, 2013 from http://www.cdc.gov/hiv/topics/surveillance/resources/reports/#supplemental.

2. UNAIDS, *Global Report: UNAIDS report on the global AIDS epidemic, 2012* (Geneva, Switzerland: Joint United Nations Programme on HIV/AIDS, 2012), accessed November 26, 2012, from http://www.unaids.org/en/media/unaids/contentassets/documents/epidemiology/2012/gr2012/20121120_UNAIDS_Global_Report_2012_en.pdf.

3. In using the term "Latinos," I am following the official nomenclature for the reporting of state statistics, even with all of the problematic, ethnicizing homogenization the term invokes. For the definitive critique of the related ethnicizing term, "Hispanics," as a useful category of analysis in AIDS risk sciences, see Merrill Singer et al., "SIDA: The economic, social, and cultural context of AIDS among Latinos," *Medical anthropology quarterly* 4 (1990): 72–114.

4. Native American HIV prevalence rates are equivalent to or slightly higher than white rates, but because of population size, Native people account for less than one half of one percent (0.4%) of total

HIV prevalence (5,000 total persons living with HIV in 2008). Asian/Pacific Islander prevalence rates are consistently 90–100 points lower than whites' and thus the lowest of all racial/ethnic groups for both men and women.

5. For critiques of "race" as a category of difference in medicine, see Lundy Braun et al., "Racial categories in medical practice: How useful are they?" *PLoS Med* 4 (2007): e271, doi: 10.1371/journal. pmed.0040271; Troy Duster, "Lessons from history: Why race and ethnicity have played a major role in biomedical research," *Journal of law, medicine and ethics* 34 (2006): 487–496; Steven Epstein, *Inclusion: The politics of difference in medical research* (Chicago: University of Chicago Press, 2007); Nancy Krieger, "Stormy Weather: Race, gene expression, and the science of health disparities," *American journal of public health* 95 (2005): 2155–2160; and Dorothy Roberts, *Fatal invention: How science, politics, and big business re-create race in the twenty-first century* (New York: The New Press, 2011).

6. Paul Farmer, "Rethinking 'emerging infectious diseases,'" *Infections and inequality: The modern plagues* (Berkeley: University of California Press, 2001), 37–58.

7. Michael Omi and Howard Winant, *Racial formation in the United States: From the 1960s to the 1990s*, second ed. (New York: Routledge, 1994).

8. Lauren Berlant, "Slow death (sovereignty, obesity, lateral agency)," *Critical Inquiry* 33 (2007): 754–780.

9. The title of this section pays homage to three key texts in the communal response and critical analysis of the AIDS epidemic. The first is *How to Have Sex in an Epidemic*, possibly the first, gay, safer-sex pamphlet, written by New York-based gay health activists Michael Callen and Richard Berkowitz (New York: News from the Front, 1983); reprinted in Richard Berkowitz, *Stayin' Alive: The invention of safe sex, A personal history* (Cambridge, MA: Westview Press, 2003), 187–223. Even though it was written in the very first months of the known epidemic, well before HIV was discovered, its common-sense prescriptions for enjoying sex and reducing risk of disease transmission made it a ground-breaking document that remains one of the very best safer-sex guides for gay men. The second is Douglas Crimp's essay, "How to have promiscuity in an epidemic" (in *AIDS: Cultural Analysis, Cultural Activism* (Cambridge: The MIT Press, 1988), 237–268). Obviously drawing upon the title of the former, Crimp's critical essay was one of the first to theorize the sexual knowledge

emerging from gay communities and its relation to efforts to suppress this knowledge. Finally, Paula Treichler's *How to have theory in an epidemic: Cultural chronicles of AIDS* (Durham: Duke University Press, 1999) is the groundbreaking cultural study of the discourses of AIDS science and public policy.

10. Elizabeth Fee and Nancy Krieger, "Understanding AIDS: Historical interpretations and the limits of biomedical individualism," *American journal of public health* 83 (October 1993): 1477–1486.

11. Nancy Krieger, "Epidemiology and the web of causation: Has anyone seen the spider?" *Social science and medicine* 39 (1994): 892.

12. While this reductionism is a strong tendency, it is challenged even within biomedicine. As will become clear, I use biomedical knowledge to argue against the reductionism and fetishism of dominant biomedical individualism in HIV risk discourses. Thus, biomedicine has produced knowledge that can be put to use, if not to the use that biomedicine might pursue.

13. Krieger, "Web of causation," 894.

14. Didier Fassin, "Embodied history: Uniqueness and exemplarity of South African AIDS," *African journal of AIDS research* 1 (2002): 65.

15. Arline T. Geronimus, "To mitigate, resist, or undo: Addressing structural influences on the health of urban populations," *American journal of public health* 90, no. 6 (2000): 867–872.

16. Office of National AIDS Policy, *National HIV/AIDS strategy for the United States* (Washington, DC: Office of National AIDS Policy, 2010), downloaded May 13, 2013, from http://www.whitehouse.gov/administration/eop/onap/nhas; Richard D. Moore, Jeanne C. Keruly, and John G. Bartlett, "Improvement in the health of HIV-infected persons in care: Reducing disparities," *Clinical infectious diseases* 55, no. 9 (2012): 1242–1251.

17. David McBride, *From TB to AIDS: Epidemics among urban blacks since 1900* (Albany: State University of New York Press, 1991); see also W. Michael Byrd and Linda A. Clayton, *An American Health Dilemma*, 2 volumes (New York: Routledge, 2000 and 2002).

18. William Edward Burghardt Du Bois, "The health and physique of the Negro American" (1906), *American journal of public health* 93 (February 2003): 276.

19. Vicente Navarro, "US Marxist scholarship in the analysis of health and medicine," *International journal of health services* 15 (1985): 526 (emphasis added).

20. Navarro, "US Marxist scholarship," 527; Frederick Engels, *The condition of the working class in England* (1845; London: Grenada Publishing, 1962).

21. Evan Stark, "The epidemic as a social event," *International journal of health services* 7, no. 4 (1977): 681–705.

22. Navarro, "US Marxist scholarship," 527.

23. The third major figure in the materialist health tradition is Rudolf Virchow, who wrote an influential account of a typhus epidemic in the Prussian province of Upper Silesia in the mid-nineteenth century; see Rex Taylor and Annelie Rieger, "Rudolf Virchow on the typhus epidemic in Upper Silesia: An introduction and translation," *Sociology of health and illness* 6, no. 2 (1984): 201–218.

24. For a useful survey of these traditions, their histories, and their distinctions, see Nancy Krieger, *Epidemiology and the people's health: Theory and context* (New York: Oxford, 2011).

25. Krieger, "Web of causation," (op cit.); see also Bruce G. Link and Jo Phelan, "Social conditions as fundamental causes of disease," *Journal of health and social behavior* 35, extra issue (1995): 80–94.

26. McBride, *From TB to AIDS*, esp. ch. 6.

27. Ibid., 159.

28. On the biomedical transition in public health and medicine, see George Rosen, *A history of public health* (1958; Baltimore, MD: The Johns Hopkins University Press, 1993); and Paul Starr, *The social transformation of American medicine* (New York: Basic Books, 1982).

29. McBride, *From TB to AIDS*, 163; see also Paul Farmer, *AIDS and accusation: Haiti and the geography of blame*, updated ed. (Berkeley: University of California Press, 2006).

30. McBride, *From TB to AIDS*, 166–169. Even McBride is not immune from the phobic relationship to black people living with AIDS. His descriptions insistently contrast white gay men with black and Hispanic drug users and their sexual partners and children. All of the homosexuals seem to be white, and all of the black people are heterosexual; the epidemic facing black gay and bisexual men is nowhere to be found in his survey of the suffering.

31. Cathy J. Cohen, *The boundaries of blackness: AIDS and the breakdown of black politics* (Chicago: University of Chicago Press, 1999).

32. Allow me to insist on the word "somewhat" in this sentence. I do not want to imply simple naivety on McBride's part. He clearly sees these three historical facts as emerging within the pressure

cooker of racism. In my reading, however, I do not see McBride coordinating the three historical factors that he so astutely identifies as an ideological prop for biomedical individualism. Rather, they seem to appear in his historical analysis as failures, or more properly, as historical defeats that allow biomedicine to hegemonize the discursive field.

33. Cindy Patton, *Sex and germs: The politics of AIDS* (Boston: South End Press, 1985); and "Heterosexual AIDS panic: A queer paradigm," *Gay community news,* February 9, 1985, 3, 6.

34. Michel de Certeau, *The practice of everyday life,* trans. Steven Rendall (Berkeley: University of California Press, 1984).

35. I owe this phrasing and distinction to Jared Sexton (personal communication). For an especially important critique of "blame the victim" ideology in HIV risk discourses, including scientific discourses, see Nina Glick Schiller, "What's wrong with this picture? The hegemonic construction of culture in AIDS research in the United States," *Medical anthropology quarterly* 6 (1992): 237–254.

36. Michel Foucault, "Governmentality," *The Foucault Effect: Studies in governmentality,* ed. Graham Burchell, Colin Gordon, and Peter Miller (Chicago: The University of Chicago Press, 1991), 87–104. One of the best treatments of Foucault's concept of governmentality as a form of problematizing is Colin Gordon's "Governmental rationality: An introduction," also in *The Foucault Effect,* 1–51.

37. Cohen, *The boundaries of blackness;* Wende Elizabeth Marshall, "AIDS, race and the limits of science," *Social science and medicine* 60 (2005): 2515–2525.

38. Gilles Bibeau and Duncan Pederson, "A return to scientific racism in medical social sciences: The case of sexuality and the AIDS epidemic in Africa," in *New horizons in medical anthropology: Essays in honor of Charles Leslie,* ed. Mark Nichter and Margaret Lock (New York: Routledge, 2002), 141–171.

39. Tony Barnett and Alan Whiteside, *AIDS in the twenty-first century: Disease and globalization,* second ed. (New York: Palgrave Macmillan, 2006).

40. Rucker C. Johnson and Steven Raphael, "The effects of male incarceration dynamics on Acquired Immune Deficiency Syndrome infection rates among African American women and men," *Journal of law and economics* 52 (2009): 251–293.

41. Keith Boykin, *Beyond the down low: Sex, lies, and denial in Black America* (New York: Carroll & Graf Publishers, 2005); Benoit

Denizet-Lewis, "Double lives on the down low," *The New York Times Magazine*, August 3, 2003. For a critical analysis, see Layli Phillips, "Deconstructing 'down low' discourse: The politics of sexuality, gender, race, AIDS, and anxiety," *Journal of African American studies* 9 (2005): 3–15.

42. CDC, "HIV among African Americans," updated March 20, 2013, accessed March 29, 2013, from http://www.cdc.gov/ hiv /topics/aa/index.htm.

43. CDC, "HIV/AIDS—Home," accessed March 29, 2013, from www.cdc.gov/hiv/.

44. CDC, "HIV prevention among injection drug users," updated September 26, 2011, accessed March 29, 2013, from http:// www.cdc.gov/idu.

45. CDC, "HIV among African Americans," op. cit.

46. Eduardo Bonilla-Silva, *Racism without racists: Color-blind racism and the persistence of racial inequality in the United States*, third ed. (Lanham, MD: Rowman & Littlefield, 2010); David Theo Goldberg, "Racism without racism," *PMLA* 123 (2008): 1712–1716.

47. Patton, "Heterosexual AIDS panic," op. cit.

48. One of the earliest people with AIDS activists, Michael Callen, challenged the facile description of early gay people with AIDS as "previously healthy." As Cindy Patton reports, Callen argued that "many gay men had chronic and repeated infections of various sexually transmitted diseases. The medical industry's general disregard for overall sexual health and the broad cultural view that STDs are the price paid for sex allow this disease history to be considered 'previously healthy.'" Cindy Patton, *Sex and germs: The politics of AIDS* (Boston: South End Press, 1985), 166, n.3. Michelle Cochrane has taken this critique even further in her research on the demographics of the earliest men to be diagnosed with AIDS in San Francisco in 1981, almost all of whom had some combination of drug addiction, homelessness, mental illness, and joblessness in their recent histories; see her, *When AIDS began: San Francisco and the making of an epidemic* (New York: Routledge, 2004).

49. CDC, "*Pneumocystis* pneumonia—Los Angeles," *MMWR* 30 (June 5, 1981): 1–3, accessed January 8, 2013, from http://www .cdc.gov/mmwr/preview/mmwrhtml/june_5.htm.

50. Michel Foucault, *The history of sexuality, volume 1: An introduction*, trans. Robert Hurley (New York: Vintage Books, 1990); see also, Gerald M. Oppenheimer, "In the eye of the storm: The

epidemiological construction of AIDS," in *AIDS: The burdens of history*, ed. Elizabeth Fee and Daniel M. Fox (Berkeley: University of California Press, 1988), 267–300.

51. Cindy Patton, *Fatal advice: How safe-sex education went wrong* (Durham: Duke University Press, 1996).

52. On the overlap between "risk groups" and the structuring of social inequality, see also Elizabeth Fee and Nancy Krieger, "Understanding AIDS: Historical interpretations and the limits of biomedical individualism," *American journal of public health* 83 (1993): 1481.

53. Foucault, *History of sexuality*, 138.

54. As Eve Kosofsky Sedgwick has demonstrated, the "drug addict" and the "homosexual" have been discursively yoked together since their common invention as subjects of their behaviors in the nineteenth century; see "Epidemics of the will," in her *Tendencies* (Durham: Duke University Press, 1993), 130–142.

55. Richard Dyer, "The role of stereotypes," in *The matter of images: Essays on representations* (New York: Routledge, 1993), 11–18. My thanks to Miranda Joseph for providing me with Dyer's essay.

56. Fassin, "Embodied history," 65.

57. I am guided in my thinking about the functionality of stereotypes by Homi Bhabha, "The other question: The stereotype and colonial discourse," in *The sexual subject: A Screen reader in sexuality*, ed. Mandy Merck (London: Routledge, 1992), 312–331.

58. Lisa Duggan, *The twilight of equality? Neoliberalism, cultural politics, and the attack on democracy* (Boston: Beacon Press, 2003).

59. Deborah Lupton argues that the primary purpose of public health education sloganeering is not to educate a public but simply to demonstrate "care" on the part of public officials. It is a relatively inexpensive way for government to do nothing to intervene in health while appearing to do something. See her *The imperative of health: Public health and the regulated body* (Thousand Oaks, CA: Sage, 1995), 125.

60. James H. Jones, *Bad Blood: The Tuskegee Syphilis Experiment* (New York: The Free Press, 1981); Dorothy Roberts, *Killing the Black body: Race, reproduction, and the meaning of liberty* (New York: Vintage Books, 1999); Stephen B. Thomas and Sandra C. Quinn, "The Tuskegee Syphilis Study, 1932 to 1972: Implications for HIV education and AIDS risk education programs in Black communities," *American journal of public health* 81 (1991): 1498–1505.

61. Cindy Patton, *Inventing AIDS* (New York: Routledge, 1990).

62. McBride, *From TB to AIDS*; see also Patton, *Inventing AIDS*, 6.

63. On liberal nonrecognition, see Kimberlé Williams Crenshaw, "Color-blind dreams and racial nightmares: Reconfiguring racism in the post-civil rights era," in *Birth of a nation'hood: Gaze, script, and spectacle in the O.J. Simpson case*, ed. Toni Morrison and Claudia Brodsky Lacour (New York: Pantheon Books, 1997), 97–168; Bonilla-Silva, *Racism without racists*; and Goldberg, "Racism without racism."

64. Cathy J. Cohen, "Punks, bulldaggers and welfare queens: The radical potential of queer politics?" *GLQ* 3 (1997): 441.

65. See especially Patricia Hill Collins, *Black sexual politics: African Americans, gender, and the new racism* (New York: Routledge, 2004); Roderick A. Ferguson, *Aberrations in Black: Toward a queer of color critique* (Minneapolis: University of Minnesota Press, 2004); Dorothy Roberts, *Killing the Black body*, op. cit.; and Dorothy Roberts, *Shattered bonds: The color of child welfare* (New York: Basic Civitas Books, 2003).

66. Cohen, "Punks," 442.

67. It should not need to be said, but probably must be said, that this is not an assertion either of black normativity or exclusive black heterosexuality. I am not claiming that black people are really normal and heterosexual, but misrepresented as queers. My argument here is that what matters for the AIDS epidemic is the state-mediated, structured violence that black people experience, a violence that is ideologically misrepresented—in a classic, blame-the-victim reversal—as black pathology. The variety of pleasures that black people pursue are, in fact, almost entirely insignificant for understanding the manner in which black people are made vulnerable to HIV.

68. Stark, "The epidemic as a social event," op. cit.

69. Roberts, *Fatal invention*.

70. Eileen Stillwaggon, *AIDS and the ecology of poverty* (New York: Oxford University Press, 2006).

71. Deborah Wallace and Roderick Wallace, *A plague on your houses: How New York was burned down and national public health crumbled* (New York: Verso, 1998).

72. Cochrane, *When AIDS began*, op. cit.; Roderick Wallace and Deborah Wallace, "U.S. apartheid and the spread of AIDS to the suburbs: A multi-city analysis of the political economy of spatial epidemic threshold," *Social science and medicine* 41 (1995): 333–345; Roderick Wallace, "Plague and power relations." *Geografiska annaler, series B: human geography* 89 (2007): 319–339.

73. Alison Katz, "AIDS, individual behaviour and the unexplained remaining variation," *African journal of AIDS research* 1 (2002): 125–142.

74. Douglas Massey and Nancy Denton, *American apartheid: Segregation and the making of the underclass* (Cambridge, MA: Harvard University Press, 1993).

75. Johnson and Raphael, "The effects of male incarceration dynamics," op. cit.

76. Michael Massoglia, "Incarceration, health, and racial disparities in health," *Law and society review* 42 (2008): 275–306.

77. Loïc Wacquant et al., "The wedding of workfare and prisonfare revisited," *Social justice* 38 (2011): 1–16.

78. Wende Elizabeth Marshall, "AIDS, race and the limits of science," *Social science and medicine* 60 (2005): 2516.

79. Geronimus, "To mitigate, resist, or undo," 868.

80. Ruth Wilson Gilmore, *Golden Gulag: Prisons, surplus, crisis, and opposition in globalizing California* (Berkeley and Los Angeles: University of California Press, 2007).

81. Berlant, "Slow death."

2 AIDS, Place, and the Embodiment of Racism

1. Wende Elizabeth Marshall, "AIDS, race and the limits of science," *Social science and medicine* 60 (2005): 2516.

2. Toni Morrison, *Playing in the dark: Whiteness and the literary imagination* (New York: Vintage Books, 1993); Michael Omi and Howard Winant, *Racial formation in the United States: From the 1960s to the 1990s*, second ed. (New York: Routledge, 1994).

3. Marshall, "AIDS, race," 2516.

4. Priscilla Wald, *Contagious: Cultures, carriers, and the outbreak narrative* (Durham: Duke University Press, 2008), 2.

5. Wald, *Contagious*, ch. 5.

6. Randy Shilts, *And the band played on: Politics, people, and the AIDS epidemic* (New York: Penguin Books, 1988), xxi.

7. Peter Gould, *The slow plague: A geography of the AIDS pandemic* (Oxford: Blackwell Publisher, 1993), 60

8. Tony Barnett and Alan Whiteside, *AIDS in the twenty-first century: Disease and globalization*, second ed. (New York: Palgrave Macmillan, 2006), 4.

9. *Rise of the Planet of the Apes*, dir. Rupert Wyatt (Twentieth Century Fox Film Corporation, 2011).

10. Denise Brehm, "New model of disease contagion ranks U.S. airports in terms of their spreading influence," *MITnews*, July 22,

2012, accessed February 18, 2013, from http://web.mit.edu /newsoffice/2012/spread-of-disease-in-airports-0723.html.

11. Wald, *Contagious*, 2, 33.

12. On the invention of "African AIDS," see Cindy Patton, "From nation to family: Containing African AIDS," in *The lesbian and gay studies reader*, ed. Henry Abelove, Michèle Aina Barale, and David Halperin (New York: Routledge, 1993), 127–138; Paula Treichler, "AIDS, Africa, and cultural theory," in *How to have theory in an epidemic: Cultural chronicles of AIDS* (Durham: Duke University Press, 1999), 205–234; Simon Watney, "Missionary positions: AIDS, 'Africa,' and race," in *Practices of freedom: Selected writings on HIV/AIDS* (Durham: Duke University Press, 1994), 103–120. Paul Farmer, *AIDS and accusation: Haiti and the geography of blame*, updated ed. (Berkeley: University of California Press, 2006). The blame Shilts assigns to Dugas demands a profound, and profoundly unfair, novelization of his life and illness. For important critiques of Shilts's representation, see Douglas Crimp, "AIDS: Cultural Analysis/Cultural Activism," in *AIDS: Cultural Analysis, Cultural Activism*, ed. Douglas Crimp (Cambridge, MA: The MIT Press, 1988), 3–16; Douglas Crimp, "Randy Schilts's miserable failure," in *Melancholia and moralism: Essays on AIDS and queer politics* (Cambridge, MA: The MIT Press, 2002), 117–128; Simon Watney, "Politics, people and the AIDS epidemic: *And the Band Played On*," in *Practices of freedom: Selected writings on HIV/AIDS* (Durham: Duke University Press, 1994), 98–100; and *Zero patience*, dir. John Greyson (Toronto: Cineplex Odeon Corporation, 1993).

13. Cindy Patton, *Fatal advice: How safe-sex education went wrong* (Durham: Duke University Press, 1996), ch. 2.

14. Cindy Patton, *Globalizing AIDS* (Minneapolis: University of Minnesota Press, 2002).

15. Gould, *The slow plague*, 62.

16. Roderick Wallace et al., "The hierarchical diffusion of AIDS and violent crime among US metropolitan regions: Inner-city decay, stochastic resonance and reversal of the mortality transition," *Social science and medicine* 44 (1997): 935.

17. Gould, *The slow plague*, 61–70, provides a very useful and readable discussion of these levels of geographic analysis for infectious disease diffusion.

18. Roderick Wallace, "Plague and power relations," *Geografiska annaler, series B: human geography* 89 (2007): 320–321.

19. For more detail, see Peter Gould, *Becoming a geographer* (Syracuse, NY: Syracuse University Press, 1999), 195–204.

20. Roderick Wallace et al., "Deindustrialization, inner-city decay, and the hierarchical diffusion of AIDS in the USA: How neoliberal and cold war policies magnified the ecological niche for emerging infections and created a national security crisis," *Environment and planning A* 31 (1999): 113–139.

21. Wallace et al., "Hierarchical diffusion," 945.

22. Wallace et al., "Deindustrialization," 125, Fig. 6.

23. Roderick Wallace and Deborah Wallace, "US apartheid and the spread of AIDS to the suburbs: A multi-city analysis of the political economy of spatial epidemic threshold," *Social science and medicine* 41 (1995): 337.

24. Wallace, "Plague," 323.

25. Wallace et al., "Hierarchical diffusion," 945.

26. US Census Bureau, *Population estimates*, July 1, 2010, accessed March 3, 2013, from http://www.census.gov/popest/data/inter censal/index.html.

27. Paul A. Jargowsky, *Poverty and place: Ghettos, barrios, and the American city* (New York: Russell Sage Foundation, 1997).

28. Wallace, "Plague," 323.

29. See especially Roderick Wallace and Robert Fullilove, "Why simple regression models work so well describing 'risk behaviors' in the USA," *Environment and planning A* 31 (1999): 719–734.

30. CDC, "HIV among African Americans," fact sheet, updated February 2013, accessed March 23, 2013, http://www.cdc.gov /hiv/pdf/risk_HIV_AAA.pdf (emphasis in original).

31. CDC, "Characteristics associated with HIV infection among heterosexuals in urban areas with high AIDS prevalence—24 cities, United States, 2006–2007," *MMWR* 60 (2011): 1045–1049.

32. CDC, "New CDC analysis reveals strong link between poverty and HIV infection," press release, July 19, 2010, accessed July 23, 2010, http://www.cdc.gov/nchhstp/newsroom/povert yandhivpressrelease.html.

33. Paul Denning and Elizabeth DiNenno, "Communities in Crisis: Is there a generalized HIV epidemic in impoverished urban areas of the United States?" poster presentation, July 18–23, 2010, *AIDS 2010: XVIII International AIDS Conference* (Vienna, Austria).

34. For a historical account of biomedicine's tendancy to transform social determinants of disease into behavioral discourse, see Dorothy Porter, "How did social medicine evolve, and where is it heading?" *PLoS Med* 3 (2006): e399, accessed December 3, 2010, doi: 10.1371/journal.pmEdited by0030399.

35. For an analysis of these spatializing practices, see Patton, *Fatal advice*, esp. ch. 2.

36. CDC, "New CDC analysis."

37. Ibid.

38. Ibid.

39. Merrill Singer, "AIDS and the health crisis of the US urban poor: The perspective of critical medical anthropology," *Social science and medicine* 39 (1994): 936–937 (emphasis in original).

40. Michael G. Marmot et al., "Employment grade and coronary heart disease in British civil servants," *Journal of epidemiology and community health* 32 (1978): 244–249; Michael G. Marmot, Martin J. Shipley, and Geoffrey Rose, "Inequalities in death: Specific explanations of a general patters?" *Lancet* 1 (1984): 1003–1006; *Unnatural causes: Is inequality making us sick?* Series created and produced by Larry Adelman and Llewellyn M. Smith (San Francisco: California Newsreel, 2008).

41. Nancy Krieger, "Theories for social epidemiology in the 21st century: An ecosocial perspective," *International journal of epidemiology* 30 (2001): 672. Krieger first introduced the term "ecosocial theory" in Nancy Krieger, "Epidemiology and the web of causation: Has anyone seen the spider?" *Social science and medicine* 39 (1994): 887–903.

42. Krieger, "Theories," 672.

43. Krieger, "Theories," 671–672.

44. Krieger, "Theories," 671.

45. Anne Fausto-Sterling, "The bare bones of sex: part 1—Sex and gender," *Signs: Journal of women in culture and society* 30 (2005): 1495.

46. Anne Fausto-Sterling, "The problem with sex/gender and nature/nurture," in *Debating biology: Sociological reflections on health, medicine, and society*, ed. S. Williams, L. Birke, and G. Brendelow (New York: Routledge, 2003), 123–132.

47. Anne Fausto-Sterling, "Refashioning race: DNA and the politics of health care," *Differences: A journal of feminist cultural studies* 15, no. 3 (2004): 31.

48. Fausto-Sterling, "Bare bones," 1511, n. 39.

49. Nancy Krieger et al., "Racism, sexism, and social class: Implications for studies of health, disease, and well-being," *American journal of preventive medicine* 9 (1993): 82. This research is rehearsed in a broadly accessible manner in the segement of *Unnatural causes* titled "When the bough breaks."

50. Krieger et al., "Racism," 82.

51. Krieger et al., "Racism," 82.

52. 14.4 per 1,000 versus 13.9 per 1,000; from Krieger et al., "Racism," 83, table 1.

53. Nancy Krieger and Stephen Sidney, "Racial discrimination and blood pressure: The Cardia study of young black and white adults," *American journal of public health* 86 (1996): 1370–1378.

54. Fausto-Sterling, "Refashioning Race," 27–28.

55. See evidence cited in Krieger et al., "Racism," esp. n. 27–29. For the definitive critique of the racial pathologization of black women for drug use in pregnancy, see Dorothy Roberts, *Killing the Black body: Race, reproduction, and the meaning of liberty* (New York: Vintage Books, 1999).

56. Quoted in Dorothy Roberts, *Fatal invention: How science, politics, and big business re-create race in the twenty-first century* (New York: The New Press, 2011), 131.

57. Roberts, *Fatal invention*, esp. 123ff.

58. Roberts, *Fatal invention*, 129.

59. Cf. Myron S. Cohen, "HIV prevention: Rethinking the risk of transmission," *IAVA report* 8 (September–November 2004): 1–4, accessed October 19, 2013, from http://www.iavireport.org /Back-Issues/Pages/IAVI-Report-08(3)-HIVPreventionRethin kingtheRiskofTransmission.aspx (cited in Barnett and Whiteside, *AIDS in the twenty-first century*, 41). Cohen suggest a much wider range of probability for each transmission category, but his only explanation for this range is viral load at different stages of HIV disease. Transmissibility is referred back to the natural history of HIV (biomedical logic), divorced from ecological context.

60. Alison Katz, "AIDS, individual behaviour and the unexplained remaining variation," *African journal of AIDS research* 1 (2002): 125–142; Eileen Stillwaggon, *AIDS and the ecology of poverty* (New York: Oxford University Press, 2006); idem., "The ecology of poverty: Nutrition, parasites, and vulnerability to HIV /AIDS," in *AIDS, poverty, and hunger: Challenges and responses*, ed. Stuart Gillespie (Washington, DC: International Food Policy Research Institute, 2006), 167–180; idem., "Complexity, cofactors, and the failure of AIDS policy in Africa," *Journal of the International AIDS Society* 12 (2009): e12, doi: 10.1186/1758-2652-12-12; and idem., "HIV transmission in Latin America: Comparison with Africa and policy implications," *South African journal of economics* 68 (2000): 985–1011. See also B. Auvert et al., "Ecological and individual level analysis of risk factors for HIV infection in four urban populations in sub-Saharan Africa with different levels of HIV infection," *AIDS* 15, Suppl 4 (2001): S15–30.

61. See also Didier Fassin, "The embodiment of inequality," *EMBO reports* 4, special issue (2003): S4–9.

62. The next two subsections, on mucosal barriers and overall immune health, draw extensively from the synthetic work done by Katz, "Unexplained," and Stillwaggon, *AIDS and the ecology of poverty*. I have, however, reorganized their descriptions around immune compromises (rather than source of compromise) and contributed additional, supporting scholarship.

63. Shehzad M. Iqbal and Rupert Kaul, "Mucosal innate immunity as a determinant of HIV susceptibility," *American journal of reproductive immunology* 59 (2008): 44–54.

64. Bill Woodward, "Protein, calories, and immune defense," *Nutrition reviews* 56, no. 1, pt. 2 (1998): S84–92.

65. See Katz, "Unexplained," 134–135, and Stillwaggon, *AIDS and the ecology of poverty*, 48–66, for reviews of the biomedical research on concurrent infection and HIV.

66. Katz, "Unexplained," 131–132; Roderick Wallace, "A synergism of plagues: 'Planned shrinkage,' contagious housing destruction, and AIDS in the Bronx," *Environmental research* 47 (1988): 1–33.

67. O. O. Oguntibeju et al., "The interrelationship between nutrition and the immune system in HIV infection: A review," *Pakistan journal of biological sciences* 10 (2007): 4327–4338.

68. Gerald T. Keusch, "The history of nutrition: Malnutrition, infection and immunity," *Journal of nutrition* 133 (2003): 336S–340S; David Sander and Abdulrahman Sambo, "AIDS in Africa: The implications of economic recession and structural adjustment," *Health policy and planning* 6 (1991): 157–165.

69. Nevin S. Scrimshaw and John Paul SanGiovanni, "Synergism of nutrition, infection, and immunity: An overview," *American journal of clinical nutrition* 66 (1997): 464S–477S.

70. William Biesel, "Nutrition and immune function: Overview," *Journal of nutrition* 126 (1996): 2611S–2615S; Ranjit Kumar Chandra, "Nutrition and the immune system: An introduction," *American journal of clinical nutrition* 66 (1997): 460S–463S.

71. David McMurray, "Impact of nutritional deficiencies on resistance to experimental pulmonary tuberculosis," *Nutrition reviews* 56, no.1, pt. 2 (1998): S147–152.

72. Susanna Cunningham-Rundles, "Analytical methods for evaluation of immune response in nutrient intervention," *Nutrition reviews* 56, no. 1, pt. 2 (1998): S27–37.

73. Chandra, "Nutrition and the immune system."

74. Scrimshaw and SanGiovanni, "Synergism of nutrition."

75. Marianna K. Baum, Gail Shor-Posner, and Adriana Campa, "Zinc status in human immunodeficiency virus infection," *Journal of*

nutrition 130, suppl 5S (2000): 1421S–1423S; Biesel, "Nutrition and immune function"; Chandra, "Nutrition and the immune system"; Cunninham-Rundles, "Analytical methods."

76. D. Malvy, "Micronutrients and tropical viral infections: One aspect of pathogenic complexity in tropical medicine," *Médécine tropicale* 59, no. 4, part 2 (1999): 442–448; Richard D. Semba, "The role of vitamin A and related retinoids in immune function," *Nutrition reviews* 56, no. 1, pt. 2 (1998): S38–48.

77. Stillwaggon, *AIDS and the ecology of poverty*, 34.

78. R. Kaul et al., "The genital tract immune milieu: An important determinant of HIV susceptibility and secondary transmission," *Journal of reproductive immunology* 77 (2008): 32–40; Gavin Morrow et al., "Current concepts of HIV transmission," *Current HIV/AIDS reports* 4 (2007): 29–35; James Wilton, "From exposure to infection: The biology of HIV transmission," *The Body: The complete HIV/AIDS resource*, last updated fall 2011, accessed May 12, 2013, http://www.thebody.com/content/68661/from-exposure-to-infection-the-biology-of-hiv-tran.html.

79. Kalpana Gupta and Per Johan Klasse, "How do viral and host factors modulate the sexual transmission of HIV? Can transmission be blocked?" *PLoS Med* 3 (2006): e79, doi: 10.1371/journal.pmed.0030079; Thomas C. Quinn et al., "Viral load and heterosexual transmission of human immunodeficiency virus type 1," *New England journal of medicine* 342 (2000): 921–929.

80. Katz, "Unexplained," 134 (emphasis in original).

81. Katz, "Unexplained," 127.

82. Paul E. M. Fine, "Herd immunity: History, theory, practice," *Epidemiologic reviews* 15 (1993): 265–302; T. Jacob John and Reuben Samuel, "Herd immunity and herd effect: New insights and definitions," *European journal of epidemiology* 16 (2000): 601–606.

83. Patton, *Fatal advice*.

84. Stillwaggon, *AIDS and the ecology of poverty*, 8.

85. Mirko D. Grmek, *History of AIDS: Emergence and origin of a modern pandemic*, trans. Russell C. Maulitz and Jacalyn Duffin (Princeton: Princeton University Press, 1990); Stephen S. Morse, "Factors in the emergence of infectious diseases," *Emerging infectious diseases* 1 (1995): 7–15; Robin A. Weiss and Anthony J. McMichael, "Social and environmental risk factors in the emergence of infectious diseases," *Nature medicine* 10 (2004): S70–76.

86. Singer, "AIDS and the health crisis of the US urban poor," 933; see also Merrill Singer and Scott Clair, "Syndemics and public

health: Reconceptualizing disease in bio-social context," *Medical anthropology quarterly* 17 (2003): 423–441.

87. Arline T. Geronimus, "To mitigate, resist, or undo: Addressing structural influences on the health of urban populations," *American journal of publich health* 90 (2000): 868.

88. Douglas Massey and Nancy Denton, *American apartheid: Segregation and the making of the underclass* (Cambridge, MA: Harvard University Press, 1993).

89. Stephen Steinberg, *Turning back: The retreat from racial justice in American thought and policy* (Boston: Beacon Press, 1995); see also Kimberlé Williams Crenshaw, "Color-blind dreams and racial nightmares: Reconfiguring racism in the post-civil rights era," in *Birth of a nation'hood: Gaze, script, and spectacle in the O.J. Simpson case*, ed. Toni Morrison and Claudia Brodsky Lacour (New York: Pantheon Books, 1997), 97–168; and Manning Marable, "Structural racism and American democracy: Historical and theoretical perspectives," *Souls: A critical journal of Black politics, culture, and society* 3 (Winter 2001): 6–24.

90. Loïc Wacquant, "Gutting the ghetto: Political censorship and conceptual retrenchment in the American debate on urban destitution," in *Globalization and the new city: Migrants, minorities and urban transformation in comparative perspective*, ed. Malcome Cross and Robert Moore (New York: Palgrave, 2002), 32–49.

91. Martha C. Ward, "A different disease: HIV/AIDS and health care for women in poverty," *Culture, medicine and psychiatry* 17 (1993): 414, quoted in Paul Farmer and Jim Yong Kim, "Introduction to the First Edition," in *Women, poverty, and AIDS: Sex, drugs, and structural violence*, ed. Paul Farmer, Margaret Connors, and Janie Simmons, second ed. (Monroe, ME: Common Courage Press, 2011), xliii.

92. Nina Glick Schiller, "What's wrong with this picture? The hegemonic construction of culture in AIDS research in the United States," *Medical anthropology quarterly* 6 (1992): 237–254.

93. My thinking on the relationship of "behaviors" to structuring conditions is informed by philosopher Slavoj Žižek's attention to the role of what he calls "subjective violence" in obfuscating structural violence; see Slavoj Žižek, *Violence* (New York: Picador, 2008).

94. CDC, "Estimated HIV incidence in the United States, 2007–2010," *HIV Surveillance Supplemental Report* 17, no. 4 (2012), accessed February 18, 2013 from http://www.cdc.gov/hiv/topics /surveillance/resources/reports/ #supplemental.

95. UNAIDS, *Global Report: UNAIDS report on the global AIDS epidemic, 2012* (Geneva, Switzerland: Joint United Nations Programme on HIV/AIDS, 2012), accessed November 26, 2012, from http://www.unaids.org/en/media/unaids/content assets/documents/epidemiology/2012/gr2012/20121120 _UNAIDS_Global_Report_2012_en.pdf.

96. Tellingly, the Obama administration's 2010 national HIV/AIDS strategy report asserts: "throughout this document we use the terms 'gay and bisexual men' and 'gay men' interchangeably, and we intend these terms to be inclusive of all men who have sex with men (MSM), even those who do not identify as gay or bisexual." While this appears to be a gesture away from homophobic euphemism, it also reverses the original impetus of the category "men who have sex with men" by returning the potential transmission behavior to a form of identity. But the ease with which behaviors are refolded into identity simply demonstrates that they had never actually escaped from identities. See Office of National AIDS Policy, *National HIV/AIDS strategy for the United States* (Washington, DC: Office of National AIDS Policy, 2010), 2, n. 15, accessed May 13, 2013, from http://www.whitehouse.gov /administration/eop/onap/nhas.

97. For a historical and theoretical account of the modern insistence on attaching forms of behavior to forms of personhood or subjectivity, see Michel Foucault, "About the concept of the 'dangerous individual' in nineteenth-century legal psychiatry," in his *Power*, ed. James D. Faubion (New York: The New Press, 2000), 176–200.

98. See especially, Patton, *Inventing AIDS* (New York: Routledge, 1990); Patton, *Fatal Advice*; and the essays collected in Douglas Crimp, ed., *AIDS: Cultural Analysis, Cultural Activism* (Cambridge: The MIT Press, 1988).

99. Stuart Marshall, "Picturing deviancy," in *Ecstatic antibodies: Resisting the AIDS mythology*, ed. Tessa Boffin and Sunil Gupta (London: Rivers Oram Press, 1990), 19–36. For a helpful account of "degeneration" as a concept and theme in Western thought, see Arthur Herman, *The Idea of Decline in Western History* (New York: The Free Press, 1997), esp. ch. 4: "Degeneration: Liberalism's Doom," 109–144.

100. Douglas Crimp, "How to have promiscuity in an epidemic," in *AIDS: Cultural Analysis, Cultural Activism*, ed. Douglas Crimp (Cambridge: The MIT Press, 1988), 237–268.

101. See especially Cindy Patton, *Fatal Advice*; Patton, *Last served? Gendering the HIV pandemic* (Bristol, PA: Taylor & Francis Inc., 1994), ch. 1 and 3; and Patton, *Globalizing AIDS*, ch. 1.

102. Tim Brown, "AIDS, risk and social governance," *Social science and medicine* 50 (2000): 1273–1284. On "responsibility" as a form of governance, see Lisa Adkins, "Risk, sexuality and economy," *British journal of sociology* 53 (2002): 19–40; Gary Kinsman, "'Responsibility' as a strategy of governance: Regulating people living with AIDS and lesbians and gay men in Ontario," *Economy and society* 25 (1996): 394–409; and Gary Kinsman, "Managing AIDS organizing: 'Consultation,' 'partnership,' and 'responsibility' as strategies of regulation," in *Organizing dissent: Contemporary social movements in theory and practice*, ed. W. K. Carroll (Toronto: Garamond Press, 1992), 213–239.

103. Dennis Altman, "Legitimation through disaster: AIDS and the gay movement," in *AIDS: The burdens of history*, ed. Elizabeth Fee and Daniel M. Fox (Berkeley: University of California Press, 1988), 301–315; Evelynn M. Hammonds, "Seeing AIDS: Race, gender, and representation," in *The gender politics of HIV/AIDS in women: Perspectives on the pandemic in the United States*, ed. Nancy Goldstein and Jennifer L. Manlowe (New York: New York University Press, 1997), 113–126.

104. See, for example, George Chauncey, *Gay New York: Gender, urban culture, and the making of the gay male world, 1890–1940* (New York: Basic Books, 1994), esp. ch. 9.

105. Michelle Cochrane, *When AIDS began: San Francisco and the making of an epidemic* (New York: Routledge, 2004).

106. Though not without its problems, Iris Marion Young's attempt to distinguish forms of oppression still stands as a useful conceptual tool; see "Five Faces of Oppression," in her *Justice and the Politics of Difference* (Princeton: Princeton University Press, 1990), 39–65.

107. Stuart Hall, "Race, articulation, and societies structured in dominance," in *Sociological theories: Race and colonialism*, ed. Colette Guillaumin (Paris: UNESCO, 1980), 305–345; Michel Foucault, *The history of sexuality, volume 1: An introduction*, trans. Robert Hurley (New York: Vintage Books, 1990).

108. Manya Magnus et al., "Elevated HIV prevalence despite lower rates of sexual risk behaviors among black men in the District of Columbia who have sex with men," *AIDS patient care and STDs* 24 (2010): 615–622; Gregorio A. Millet et al., "Greater risk for HIV infection of black men who have sex with men: A critical literature review," *American journal of public health* 96 (2006): 1007–1019.

109. Gregorio A. Millet and John L. Peterson, "The known hidden epidemic: HIV/AIDS among black men who have sex with men in the United States," *Americal journal of preventive medicine* 32 (2007): S31–33; and Gregorio A. Millet et al., "Explaining disparities in

HIV infection among black and white men who have sex with men: A meta-analysis of HIV risk behaviors," *AIDS* 21 (2007): 2083–2091; see also Adaora A. Adimore and Victor J. Schoenbach, "Social context, sexual networks, and racial disparities in rates of sexually transmitted infections," *The journal of infectious diseases* 191 (2005): S115–122. Alternately, racially exclusive sexual networks are offered as a protective explanation for lower HIV prevalence among Asian and Pacific Islander MSM; see Chongyi Wei et al., "Lower HIV prevalence among Asian/Pacific Islander men who have sex with men: A critical review for possible reasons," *AIDS and behavior* 15 (2011): 535–649.

110. For a similar critique of sexual network studies in southern Africa, see Larry Sawers and Eileen Stillwaggon, "Concurrent sexual partnerships do not explain the HIV epidemics in Africa: A systematic review of the evidence," *Journal of the International AIDS Society* 13 (2010): e34, doi: 10.1186/1758-2652-13-34.

3 Mass Incarceration and the Black AIDS Epidemic

1. Evan Stark, "The epidemic as a social event," *International journal of health services* 7 (1977): 687–688.

2. I recognize that both race and sex are problematic demographic categories, and in particular, I want to note the way that sex functions to cover over gendered difference in HIV demographic data. To my knowledge, transgender and transsexual people are counted in this demographic data by the sex with which they were assigned at birth. Thus I want to insist on the definitional violence of race and gender in this data even as I attempt to mobilize critical resources for reading into and through them. These demographic categories provide ammunition for identifying forms of structured violence that come to bear on people in differentiated ways that are often obscured by naturalizing race and sex. We must read critically and against the grain, but at present, we have little in the way of better demographic information for getting at structured violence, other than its embodiment as race and sex.

3. Paul Farmer, *Infections and inequalities: The modern plagues* (Berkeley: University of California Press, 2001); Alison Katz, "AIDS, individual behaviour and the unexplained remaining variation," *African journal of AIDS research* 1 (2002): 125–142; Colleen O'Manique, *Neoliberalism and AIDS epidemic in Sub-Saharan Africa: Globalization's pandemic* (New York: Palgrave Macmillan, 2004); Eileen Stillwaggon, *AIDS and the ecology of poverty* (New York: Oxford University Press, 2006).

4. Tony Barnett and Alan Whiteside, *AIDS in the twenty-first century: Disease and globalization*, second ed. (New York: Palgrave Macmillan, 2006), 86.

5. Barnett and Whiteside, *AIDS in the twenty-first century*, 87.

6. Barnett and Whiteside, *AIDS in the twenty-first century*, 86.

7. Saidiya Hartman, *Lose your mother: A journey along the Atlantic slave route* (New York: Farrar, Straus and Giroux, 2007), 6.

8. Jared Sexton and Elizabeth Lee, "Figuring the prison: Prerequisites of torture at Abu Ghraib," *Antipode* 38 (2006): 1005–1022.

9. Research is desperately needed to understand what relations pertain between the AIDS epidemic and other people subject to intensified policing and incarceration, particularly through the expanded incarceration of undocumented migrants in the wars on drugs and terror. For some suggestions, see Rucker C. Johnson and Steven Raphael, "The effects of male incarceration dynamics on Acquired Immune Deficiency Syndrome infection rates among African American women and men," *Journal of law and economics* 52 (2009): esp. 270–271.

10. The Sentencing Project, "The Sentencing Project news—Incarceration," *The Sentencing Project*, n.d., accessed December 27, 2011, http://www.sentencingproject.org/template/page.cfm?id=107.

11. Thomas P. Bonczar, "Prevalence of imprisonment in the U.S. population, 1974–2001," Bureau of Justice Statistics Special Report, NCJ 197976 (U.S. Department of Justice, 2003), accessed August 14, 2011, http://bjs.ojp.usdoj.gov/content/pub/pdf/piusp01.pdf.

12. This paragraph draws heavily from Loïc Wacquant, "Deadly symbiosis: When ghetto and prison meet and mesh," *Punishment & society* 3 (2001): 96.

13. Marc Mauer and Ryan S. King, "Uneven justice: State rates of incarceration by race and ethnicity," *The Sentencing Project*, last updated 2007, accessed December 27, 2011, http://www.sentencingproject.org/doc/publications/rd_stateratesofincbyraceandethnicity.pdf.

14. Wacquant, "Deadly symbiosis," 96.

15. Becky Pettit and Bruce Western, "Mass imprisonment and the life course: Race and class inequality in U.S. incarceration," *American sociological review* 69 (2004): 151–169.

16. On racial/ethnic differences in crime and sentencing, see Gary Lefree et al., "Race and crime in post-war America: Determinants of African American and white rates, 1957–1988," *Criminology* 30 (1992): 157–188; and Robert J. Sampson and Janet R.

Lauritson, "Racial and ethnic disparities in crime and criminal justice in the United States," in *Ethnicity, crime, and immigration: Comparative and cross-national perspectives*, ed. Michael Tonry (Chicago: University of Chicago Press, 1997), 311–374 (both cited in Wacquant, "Deadly symbiosis," op cit.). On the nonrelation between incarceration rates and crime rates, see Marc Mauer and The Sentencing Project, *Race to incarcerate*, second ed. (New York: The New Press, 2006).

17. Wacquant, "Deadly symbiosis," 97.

18. Loïc Wacquant, "From slavery to mass incarceration: Rethinking the 'race question' in the US," *New left review* 13 (2002): 41.

19. Ibid. 41–42.

20. For examples, see Angela Y. Davis, *Are prisons obsolete?* (New York: Seven Stories Press, 2003); the essays collected in Joy James, ed., *Warfare in the American homeland: Policing and prison in a penal democracy* (Durham: Duke University Press, 2007); Manning Marable, "Structural racism and American democracy: Historical and theoretical perspectives," *Souls: A critical journal of Black politics, culture, and society* 3 (Winter 2001): 6–24.

21. Ruth Wilson Gilmore, *Golden Gulag: Prisons, surplus, crisis, and opposition in globalizing California* (Berkeley and Los Angeles: University of California Press, 2007).

22. Wacquant, "From slavery to mass incarceration," 48.

23. Ibid. 49.

24. Kim M. Blankenship et al., "Black-white disparities in HIV/AIDS: The role of drug policy and the corrections system," *Journal of health care for the poor and underserved* 16 (2005): 140–156; P. Estébanez et al., "The role of prisons in the HIV epidemic among female injecting drug users," *AIDS care* 14 (2002): 95–104; Johnson and Raphael, "The effects of male incarceration"; Sandra D. Lane et al., "Structural violence and racial disparity in HIV transmission," *Journal of health care for the poor and underserved* 15 (2004): 319–335; and Vickie L. Shavers and Brenda S. Shavers, "Racism and health inequality among Americans," *Journal of the national medical association* 98 (2006): 386–396.

25. Sexton and Lee, "Figuring the prison," 1006.

26. Ibid.

27. Johnson and Raphael, "The effects of male incarceration," 278.

28. The effect of incarceration on AIDS diagnosis begins in year four but is most pronounced in years nine through eleven. It ends after year thirteen. The standard HIV/AIDS incubation period prior to 1996 was thought to be five to ten years. It changed in 1996

with the introduction of antiretroviral drugs, which dramatically extended the period between HIV infection and AIDS diagnosis for those able to access the drugs.

29. Johnson and Raphael, "The effects of male incarceration," 251.
30. Bruce G. Link and Jo Phelan, "Social conditions as fundamental causes of disease," *Journal of health and social behavior* 35, extra issue (1995): 80–94; Dorothy Porter, "How did social medicine evolve, and where is it heading?" *PLoS Med* 3 (2006): e399, accessed December 3, 2010, doi: 10.1371/journal.pmEdited by0030399.
31. Wacquant, "Deadly symbiosis," 97 (emphasis in original).
32. Todd R. Clear, *Imprisoning communities: How mass incarceration makes disadvantaged neighborhoods worse* (New York: Oxford University Press, 2007), cited in Jason Schnittker et al., "Incarceration and the health of the African American community," *Du Bois Review* 8 (2011): 5.
33. Martin Y. Iguchi et al., "How criminal system racial disparities may translate into health disparities," *Journal of health care for the poor and underserved* 16, no. 4, suppl. B (2005): 48–56; Sara Wakefield and Christopher Uggen, "Incarceration and stratification," *Annual review of sociology* 36 (2010): 387–406; Christopher Wildeman, "(Mass) imprisonment and (inequities in) health," *American journal of epidemiology* 173 (2011): 488–491; and Christopher Wildeman, "Imprisonment and (inequality in) population health," University of Kentucky Center for Poverty Research Discussion Paper Series, DP2010–12. 2010, accessed September 11, 2011, http://www.ukcpr.org/Publications/DP2010–12.pdf.
34. Schnittker et al., "Incarceration and the health of the African American community," 2.
35. Michael Massoglia, "Incarceration, health, and racial disparities in health," *Law & society review* 42 (2008): 292.
36. Ibid.
37. Rashad Shabazz, "Mapping black bodies for disease: Prisons, migration, and the politics of HIV/AIDS," in *Beyond walls and cages: Prisons, borders, and global crisis*, ed. Jenna M. Loyd, Matt Mitchelson, and Andrew Burridge (Athens, GA: University of Georgia Press, 2012), 293.
38. Laura M. Maruschak and Allen J. Beck, "Medical problems of inmates," Bureau of Justice Statistics Special Report, NCJ 181644 (U.S. Department of Justice, 2001), cited in Andrew S. London and Nancy A. Myers, "Race, incarceration, and health: A life-course approach," *Research on aging* 28 (2006): 409–422.

39. Megan Comfort, "Punishment beyond the legal offender," *Annual review of law and social science* 3 (2007): 271–296.

40. Michael Massoglia and Jason Schnittker, "No real release," *Contexts* 8 (2009): 38–42, accessed September 11, 2011, www. contexts.org.

41. Marc Mauer and Meda Chesney-Lind, eds, *Invisible punishment: The collateral consequences of mass imprisonment* (New York: The New Press, 2002).

42. Shabbaz, "Mapping black bodies for disease," 296.

43. Mauer and King, "Uneven justice," 15.

44. Arline T. Geronimus, "To mitigate, resist, or undo: Addressing structural influences on the health of urban populations," *American journal of public health* 90 (2000): 867–872.

45. Mark D. Hayward et al., "The significance of socioeconomic status in explaining the racial gap in chronic health conditions," *American sociological review* 65 (2000): 910–930.

46. Lauren Berlant, "Slow death (sovereignty, obesity, lateral agency)," *Critical Inquiry* 33 (2007): 754–780.

47. Johnson and Raphael, "The effects of male incarceration," 267–268.

48. Loïc Wacquant et al., "The wedding of workfare and prisonfare revisited," *Social justice* 38 (2011): 1.

49. Wacquant et al., "The wedding of workfare," 2, 1.

50. Wacquant, "Deadly symbiosis," 97.

51. Mimi Abramovitz, "Welfare reform in the United States: Gender, race and class matter," *Critical social policy* 26 (2006): 336–364; Randy Albelda and Ann Withorn, eds, *Lost ground: Welfare reform, poverty and beyond* (Cambridge, MA: South End Press, 2002).

4   Representing Global AIDS: Africa, Heterosexuality, Violence

1. Didier Fassin, "Embodied history: Uniqueness and exemplarity of South African AIDS," *African journal of AIDS research* 1 (2002): 63–64.

2. Ibid., 64.

3. Ibid.

4. For an especially eloquent and careful account of South African resistance to the biomedical reduction of AIDS, see Didier Fassin, *When bodies remember: Experience and politics of AIDS in South Africa*, trans. Amy Jacobs and Gabrielle Varro (Berkeley: University of California Press, 2007); see also Deborah Mindry,

"Neoliberalism, activism, and HIV/AIDS in postapartheid South Africa," *Social Text* 94 (Spring 2008): 75–93. For a further analysis of the bad-faith alignment between biomedicine and global capitalism in the context of AIDS in southern Africa, see Adam Sitze, "Denialism," *The South Atlantic quarterly* 103 (2004): 769–811.

5. UNAIDS, *Global Report: UNAIDS report on the global AIDS epidemic, 2012* (Geneva, Switzerland: Joint United Nations Programme on HIV/AIDS, 2012), accessed November 26, 2012, from http://www.unaids.org/en/media /unaids/contentassets/documents/epidemiology/2012/gr2012 /20121120_UNAIDS_Global_Report_2012_en.pdf.

6. Colleen O'Manique, *Neoliberalism and AIDS epidemic in Sub-Saharan Africa: Globalization's pandemic* (New York: Palgrave Macmillan, 2004).

7. Eileen Stillwaggon, *AIDS and the ecology of poverty* (New York: Oxford University Press, 2006). The survey of racism in the science of African AIDS appears in ch. 7: "Racial Metaphors: Interpreting Sex and AIDS in Africa."

8. Paul Farmer, Margaret Connors, and Janie Simmons, eds, *Women, poverty, and AIDS: Sex, drugs, and structural violence*, second ed. (Monroe, ME: Common Courage Press, 2011).

9. Paul Farmer and Jim Yong Kim, "Introduction to the first edition," in *Women, poverty, and AIDS*, xliii.

10. This now-famous phrase appears as the title of Chapter 5 of Frantz Fanon, *Black Skin, White Masks*, trans. Charles Lam Markmann (New York: Grove Weidenfeld, 1967).

11. Wende Elizabeth Marshall, "AIDS, race and the limits of science," *Social science and medicine* 60 (2005): 2516; Jared Sexton, *Amalgamation schemes: Antiblackness and the critique of multiracialism* (Minneapolis: University of Minnesota Press, 2008), 40.

12. O'Manique, *Neoliberalism and AIDS epidemic*, 26.

13. Marc Epprecht, *Heterosexual Africa? The history of an idea from the age of exploration to the age of AIDS* (Athens, OH: Ohio State University Press, 2008).

14. O'Manique, notably, offers no evidence for her breakdown of transmission routes.

15. Epprecht, *Heterosexual Africa*, 116.

16. Epprecht, *Heterosexual Africa*, 2; internal reference to J. Phillipe Rushton, *Race, evolution and behavior: A life history perspective* (New Brunswick, NJ: Transaction, 1997), esp. 178–183.

17. See especially Cindy Patton, "From nation to family: Containing African AIDS," in *The lesbian and gay studies reader*, ed. Henry Abelove, Michèle Aina Barale, and David Halperin (New York: Routledge, 1993), 127–138; Paula Treichler, "AIDS, Africa, and cultural theory," in *How to have theory in an epidemic: Cultural chronicles of AIDS* (Durham: Duke University Press, 1999), 205–234; and Simon Watney, "Missionary positions: AIDS, 'Africa,' and race," in *Practices of freedom: Selected writings on HIV/AIDS* (Durham: Duke University Press, 1994), 103–120.

18. Cindy Patton, *Globalizing AIDS* (Minneapolis: University of Minnesota Press, 2002), Ch. 3. For examples, see Peter Piot et al., "AIDS: An international perspective," *Science* 239 (1988): 573–579, accessed July 25, 2013, from www.sciencemag.org; and Peter Piot et al., "The global epidemiology of HIV infection: Continuity, heterogeneity, and change," *Journal of acquired immune deficiency syndrome* 3 (1990): 403–412.

19. Indeed, the critique of exclusive African heterosexuality in the regional pandemic is nearly as old as the discourse asserting it; see references in note 17.

20. Cindy Patton, "Heterosexual AIDS panic: A queer paradigm," *Gay community news*, February 9, 1985, 3.

21. Quoted in Patton, "Heterosexual," 3.

22. Ibid.

23. Ibid.

24. On immunitary logic, see Roberto Esposito, *Bios: Biopolitics and philosophy*, trans. Timothy Campbell (Minneapolis: University of Minnesota Press, 2008).

25. See especially her *Last Served*, 10–12. Patton's position is nearly unique in feminist AIDS criticism. Almost all other feminist accounts of the AIDS epidemic insist that women were invisible in the early years of the AIDS epidemic and in its initial discursive construction, functionally erasing the very early appearance of sex workers, female drug users, and women who were partners of drug users, many of whom were black women. Equally damning, this scholarship has missed the force of the fantasy of "true heterosexuality," with all of its sexual, classed, and white normativity. Unfortunately in this scholarship, representation has been treated as only a matter of the presence or absence of speaking subjects, neglecting the way that representational presence in AIDS risk discourse has always been in the form of deviance.

26. Nancy Scheper-Hughes, "AIDS and the social body," *Social science and medicine* 39 (1994): 991–1003. For accounts of the notoriety of her essay and of critical responses to it, see citations listed in her text, p. 1003, n. 3.

27. Scheper-Hughes, "AIDS and the social body," 992.

28. Ibid., 996.

29. See Patton, *Last Served*, 50–59, for detailed deconstructions of the terms "sex worker" and "IV drug user," especially as they organize knowledge about women's HIV risks.

30. Nina Glick Schiller, Stephen Crystal, and Denver Lewellen, "Risky business: An examination of the cultural construction of AIDS risk groups." *Social science and medicine* 38 (1994): 1337–1346; Tim Rhodes, "The 'risk environment:' A framework for understanding and reducing drug-related harm," *International journal of drug policy* 13 (2002): 85–94.

31. One part of the brilliance of Patton's *Last Served* is that it rigorously and definitively refuses both of these false stereotypes when considering women's HIV risks in both developed and developing nations.

32. Scheper-Hughes, "AIDS and the social body," 996.

33. Edward King, *Safety in numbers: Safer sex and gay men*, forward by Cindy Patton (New York: Routledge, 1993); Walt Odets, "On the need for a gay reconstruction of public health," in *A Queer World*, ed. Martin Duberman (New York: New York University Press, 1997), 668–676.

34. Scheper-Hughes, "AIDS and the social body," 993.

35. Katz, "Unexplained," 129–130 (emphasis in original). For the classic deconstruction of the figure of the passive, dependent, "Third World woman" in Western feminist scholarship, see Chandra Talpade Mohanty, "Under western eyes: Feminist scholarship and colonial discourses," in *Third world women and the politics of feminism*, ed. Chandra Talpade Mohanty, Ann Russo, and Lourdes Torres (Bloomington: Indiana University Press, 1991), 51–80.

36. A key and highly recommended text in this tradition is the volume edited by Merrill Singer, *The political economy of AIDS* (Amityville, NY: Baywood Publishing Company, Inc., 1998).

37. For example, Stillwaggon, *AIDS and the ecology of poverty*, 17–27.

38. Katz, "Unexplained," 128.

39. Adam Geary, "Inessential theory: Culture and AIDS risk governance," *Eä: Journal of medical humanities and social studies of science and technology* 2 (April 2011), www.ea-journal.com.

40. Rhodes, "Risk environment."
41. Stillwaggon, *AIDS and the ecology of poverty*, 5.
42. Ibid., Ch. 6; see also Tim Rhodes and Milena Simic, "Transition and the HIV risk environment," *BMJ* 331 (2005): 220–223.
43. Stillwaggon, *AIDS and the ecology of poverty*, 88–89.
44. For another example, if much better contextualized, see Katz, "Unexplained," 128, in which she distinguishes between "those who take risks and those who, for various reasons, are exposed to risks taken by others."
45. See especially, Angela Davis, *Women, race & class* (New York: Vintage Books, 1983); bell hooks, *Ain't I a Woman: Black women and feminism* (Boston: South End Press, 1981); Audre Lorde, *Sister outsider: Essays and speeches* (Berkeley: Crossing Press, 1984); Kimberlé Williams Crenshaw, "Demarginalizing the intersections of race and sex: A Black feminist critique of anti-discrimination doctrine, feminist theory and antiracist politics," *University of Chicago legal forum* 4 (1989): 139–167.
46. On what he calls "the ruse of analogy," see Frank B. Wilderson III, *Red, white & black: Cinema and the structure of U.S. antagonisms* (Durham: Duke University Press, 2010), Ch. 1.
47. Dennis Altman, "Globalization, political economy, and HIV/AIDS," *Theory and Society* 28 (1999): 559–584; Tony Barnett and Alan Whiteside, *AIDS in the twenty-first century: Disease and globalization*, second ed. (New York: Palgrave Macmillan, 2006).
48. On the relationship between the neoliberal assault on public health and the global AIDS pandemic, see Rick Rowden, *The deadly ideas of neoliberalism* (New York: Zed Books, 2009).
49. See, for example, UNAIDS, *Global Report 2012*.
50. Neil Smith, "The satanic geographies of globalization: Uneven development in the 1990s," *Public culture* 10, no. 1 (1997): 174.
51. Smith, "Satanic geographies," 180.
52. Ibid. 178–179.
53. Sexton, *Amalgamation Schemes*, 40.
54. Ibid.
55. Smith, "Satanic geographies," 187.
56. See, for example, João Biehl, *Vita: Life in a zone of social abandonment* (Berkeley: University of California Press, 2005); Paul Farmer, *AIDS and accusation: Haiti and the geography of blame* (Berkeley: University of California Press, 2006); Scheper-Hughes, "AIDS and the social body."

57. Saidiya Hartman, *Lose your mother: A journey along the Atlantic slave route* (New York: Farrar, Straus and Giroux, 2007), 6.
58. Smith, "Satanic geographies," 187.
59. Jared Sexton, "People-of-color-blindness: Notes on the afterlife of slavery," *Social Text* 28 (2010): 31–56.
60. Catherine Campbell and Brian Williams, "Beyond the biomedical and behavioural: Towards an integrated approach to HIV prevention in the Southern African mining industry," *Social science and medicine* 48 (1999): 1625–1639.
61. Pace Campbell and Williams; see Katz, "Unexplained," 127, and Brooke Grundfest Schoepf, "AIDS in Africa: Structure, agency, and risk," in *HIV & AIDS in Africa: Beyond epidemiology*, ed. Ezekiel Kalipeni, Susan Craddock, Joseph R. Oppong, and Jayati Ghosh (Malden, MA: Blackwell Publishing, 2004), 123.
62. Matthew Smallman-Raynor and Andrew Cliff, *War epidemics: An historical geography of infectious diseases in military conflict and civil strife, 1850–2000* (Oxford University Press, 2004).
63. Nana K. Poku, "Africa's AIDS crisis in context: 'How the poor are dying,'" *Third world quarterly* 22 (2001): 195. Katz reports that 90 percent of women in Berlin were estimated to have had STIs in the late 1940s; see Katz, "Unexplained," 139, n. 12.
64. O'Manique, *Neoliberalism and AIDS epidemic*; Sandro Accorsi et al., "The disease profile of poverty: Morbidity and mortality in northern Uganda in the context of war, population displacement and HIV/AIDS," *Transactions of the Royal Society of Tropical Medicine and Hygiene* 99 (2005): 226–233; Maryinez Lyons, "Mobile populations and HIV/AIDS in East Africa," in *HIV & AIDS in Africa*, esp. 186–189; Matthew R. Smallman-Raynor and Andrew D. Cliff, "Civil war and the spread of AIDS in Central Africa," *Epidemiology and infection* 107 (1991): 69–80.
65. Mariella Baldo and Antonio Jorge Cabral, "Low intensity wars and social determination of the HIV transmission: The search for a new paradigm to guide research and control of the HIV-AIDS pandemic," *Action on AIDS in Southern Africa—Proceedings of Maputo Conference on Health in Transition in Southern Africa*, ed. Z. Stein and A. Zwi (New York: Columbia University Press, 1990), 40.
66. Brooke Grundfest Schoepf, "AIDS, history, and struggles over meaning," in *HIV & AIDS in Africa*; see also Joia Mukherjee, "Preface to the second edition," in *Women, poverty, and AIDS:*

Sex, drugs, and structural violence, ed. Paul Farmer, Margaret Connors, and Janie Simmons, second ed. (Monroe, ME: Common Courage Press, 2011), xi–xii.

67. Máire A Connolly and David L. Heymann, "Deadly comrades: War and infectious diseases," *The Lancet* 360 (2002): s23.

68. See, for instance, Eric A. Feldman and Ronald Bayer, eds, *Blood feuds: AIDS, blood, and the politics of medical disaster* (New York: Oxford University Press, 1999); William H. Schneider and Earnest Drucker, "Blood transfusions in the early years of AIDS in Sub-Saharan Africa," *American journal of public health* 96 (June 2006): 984–994; David Gisselquist, "Estimating HIV-1 transmission efficiency through unsafe medical injections," *International journal of STD & AIDS* 13 (2002): 152–159; David Gisselquist et al., "HIV infections in Sub-Saharan Africa not explained by sexual or vertical transmission," *International journal of STD & AIDS* 13 (2002): 657–666; and Scheper-Hughes, "AIDS and the social body."

69. Stillwaggon, *AIDS and the ecology of poverty*, 43.

70. Edward Hooper, *The river: A journey to the source of HIV and AIDS* (New York: Little, Brown and Company, 1999).

71. Patton, *Globalizing AIDS*, 61.

72. Evan Stark, "The epidemic as a social event," *International journal of health services* 7 (1977): 687–688.

Conclusion   The Politics of Crisis

1. Lauren Berlant, *Cruel optimism* (Durham: Duke University Press, 2011), 95.

2. Michel Foucault, *The history of sexuality, volume 1: An introduction*, trans. Robert Hurley (New York: Vintage Books, 1990), 138.

3. Berlant, *Cruel optimism*, 64.

4. Ibid., 100.

5. Ibid.

6. Ibid., 101.

7. Ibid.

8. Ibid., 97.

9. Michel Foucault, "*Society must be defended:*" *Lectures at the Collège de France, 1975–1976*, trans. David Macey (New York: Picadore, 2003), 243–244.

10. Ibid., 244.

11. Berlant, *Cruel optimism*, 97.
12. Sheena Asthana, "The relevance of place in HIV transmission and prevention: The commercial sex industry in Madras," in *Putting health into place: Landscape, identity, and well-being*, ed. Robin A. Kearns and Wilbert M. Gesler (Syracuse, NY: Syracuse University Press, 1998), 169.
13. Allan M. Brandt, *No magic bullet: A social history of venereal disease in the United States since 1880*, expanded ed. (New York: Oxford University Press, 1987).
14. Sylvia Noble Tesh, *Hidden arguments: Political ideology and disease prevention policy* (New Brunswick, NJ: Rutgers University Press, 1994); see also Evan Stark, "Doctors in spite of themselves: The limits of radical health criticism," *International journal of health services* 12 (1982): 419–457. While I follow Tesh's argument about the underlying ideology of disease prevention policy, we disagree on the virtue of arguing for poverty and structural factors as fundamental. To her credit, however, she understands this disagreement as essentially political, about the ideal form of social governance. She is a liberal; I am a leftist.
15. Tim Brown, "AIDS, risk and social governance," *Social science and medicine* 50 (2000): 1273–1284; Adam Geary, "Culture as an object of ethical governance in aids prevention," *Cultural studies* 21 (2007): 672–694.
16. Simon Watney, "AIDS, 'moral panic' theory, and homophobia," in *Practices of freedom: Selected writings on HIV/AIDS* (Durham: Duke University Press, 1994), 3–14.
17. Cindy Patton, *Inventing AIDS* (New York: Routledge, 1990).
18. Alondra Nelson, *Body and soul: The Black Panther party and the fight against medical discrimination* (Minneapolis: University of Minnesota Press, 2011), 22.
19. Walter Benjamin, "Theses on the philosophy of history," in *Illuminations,* ed. Hannah Arendt, trans. Harry Zohn (New York: Schocken Books, 1968), 257.

Bibliography

Abramovitz, Mimi. "Welfare reform in the United States: Gender, race and class matter." *Critical social policy* 26 (2006): 336–364.

Accorsi, Sandro, Massimo Fabiani, Barbara Nattabi, Bruno Corrado, Robert Iriso, Emingtone O. Ayella, Bongomin Pido, Paul A. Onek, Martin Ogwang, and S. Declich. "The disease profile of poverty: Morbidity and mortality in northern Uganda in the context of war, population displacement and HIV/AIDS." *Transactions of the Royal Society of Tropical Medicine and Hygiene* 99 (2005): 226–233.

Adimore, Adaora A. and Victor J. Schoenbach. "Social context, sexual networks, and racial disparities in rates of sexually transmitted infections." *The journal of infectious diseases* 191 (2005): S115–S122.

Adkins, Lisa. "Risk, sexuality and economy." *British journal of sociology* 53 (2002): 19–40.

Albelda, Randy and Ann Withorn, eds. *Lost ground: Welfare reform, poverty and beyond.* Cambridge, MA: South End Press, 2002.

Altman, Dennis. "Legitimation through disaster: AIDS and the gay movement." In *AIDS: The burdens of history*, edited by Elizabeth Fee and Daniel M. Fox, 301–315. Berkeley: University of California Press, 1988.

———. "Globalization, political economy, and HIV/AIDS." *Theory and society* 28 (1999): 559–584.

———. *Global Sex.* Chicago: University of Chicago Press, 2001.

Aral, Sevgi O., Adaora A. Adimora, and Kevin A. Fenton. "Understanding and responding to disparities in HIV and other sexually transmitted infections in African Americans." *Lancet* 372 (2008): 337–340.

Asthana, Sheena. "The relevance of place in HIV transmission and prevention: The commercial sex industry in Madras." In *Putting health into place: Landscape, identity, and well-being*, ed. Robin A. Kearns and Wilbert M. Gesler, 168–190. Syracuse, NY: Syracuse University Press, 1998.

Auerbach, David M., William W. Darrow, Harold W. Jaffe, and James W. Curran. "Cluster of cases of the acquired immune deficiency syndrome: Patients linked by sexual contact." *American journal of medicine* 76 (1984): 487–492.

Auvert, B., A. Buvé, B. Ferry, M. Caraël, L. Morison, E. Lagarde, N. J. Robinson, M. Kahindo, J. Chege, N. Rutenberg, R. Musonda, M. Laourou, and E. Akam. "Ecological and individual level analysis of risk factors for HIV infection in four urban populations in sub-Saharan Africa with different levels of HIV infection." *AIDS* 15, suppl 4 (2001): S15–S30.

Baldo, Mariella and Antonio Jorge Cabral. "Low intensity wars and social determination of the HIV transmission: The search for a new paradigm to guide research and control of the HIV-AIDS pandemic." In *Action on AIDS in Southern Africa—Proceedings of Maputo Conference on health in transition in Southern Africa*, edited by Zena Stein and Anthony B. Zwi, 34–45. New York: Columbia University Press, 1990.

Barnett, Tony and Alan Whiteside. *AIDS in the twenty-first century: Disease and globalization*. Second edition. New York: Palgrave Macmillan, 2006.

Baum, Marianna K., Gail Shor-Posner, and Adriana Campa. "Zinc status in human immunodeficiency virus infection." *Journal of nutrition* 130, suppl 5S (2000): 1421S–1423S.

Benjamin, Walter. "Theses on the philosophy of history." In *Illuminations: Essays and reflections*, edited and with an introduction by Hannah Arendt, 253–264. Translated by Harry Zohn. New York: Schocken Books, 1968.

Berkowitz, Richard. *Stayin' Alive: The invention of safe sex, A personal history*. Cambridge, MA: Westview Press, 2003.

Berlant, Lauren. "Slow death (sovereignty, obesity, lateral agency)." *Critical Inquiry* 33 (2007): 754–780.

———. *Cruel optimism*. Durham: Duke University Press, 2011.

Bhabha, Homi. "The other question: The stereotype and colonial discourse." In *The sexual subject: A Screen reader in sexuality*, edited by Mandy Merck, 312–331. London: Routledge, 1992.

Bibeau, Gilles and Duncan Pederson. "A return to scientific racism in medical social sciences: The case of sexuality and the AIDS epidemic in Africa." In *New horizons in medical anthropology: Essays in honor of Charles Leslie*, edited by Mark Nichter and Margaret Lock, 141–171. New York: Routledge, 2002.

Biehl, João. *Vita: Life in a zone of social abandonment*. Berkeley: University of California Press, 2005.

Biesel, William. "Nutrition and immune function: Overview." *Journal of nutrition* 126 (1996): 2611S–2615S.

Blankenship, Kim M., Amy B. Smoyer, Sarah J. Bray, and Kristin Mattocks. "Black-white disparities in HIV/AIDS: The role of drug policy and the corrections system." *Journal of health care for the poor and underserved* 16 (2005): 140–156.

Bonczar, Thomas P. "Prevalence of imprisonment in the U.S. population, 1974–2001." Bureau of Justice Statistics Special Report, NCJ 197976. U.S. Department of Justice, 2003. Accessed August 14, 2011. http://bjs.ojp.usdoj.gov/content/pub/pdf/piusp01.pdf.

Bonilla-Silva, Eduardo. *Racism without racists: Color-blind racism and the persistence of racial inequality in the United States.* Third edition. Lanham, MD: Rowman & Littlefield, 2010.

Boykin, Keith. *Beyond the down low: Sex, lies, and denial in Black America.* New York: Carroll & Graf Publishers, 2005.

Brandt, Allan M. *No magic bullet: A social history of venereal disease in the United States since 1880.* Expanded edition. New York: Oxford University Press, 1987.

Braun, Lundy, Anne Fausto-Sterling, Duana Fullwiley, Evelynn M. Hammonds, Alondra Nelson, William Quivers, Susan M. Reverby, and Alexandra E. Shields. "Racial categories in medical practice: How useful are they?" *PLoS Med* 4 (2007): e271, doi: 10.1371/journal.pmed.0040271.

Brehm, Denise. "New model of disease contagion ranks U.S. airports in terms of their spreading influence." *MITnews*, July 22, 2012. Accessed February 18, 2013. http://web.mit.edu/newsoffice/2012/spread-of-disease-in-airports-0723.html.

Brown, Tim. "AIDS, risk and social governance." *Social science and medicine* 50 (2000): 1273–1284.

Burchell, Graham, Colin Gordon, and Peter Miller, eds. *The Foucault Effect: Studies in governmentality.* Chicago: The University of Chicago Press, 1991.

Byrd, W. Michael and Linda A. Clayton. *An American health dilemma.* Volume One: *A medical history of African Americans and the problem of race: Beginnings to 1900.* New York: Routledge, 2000.

———. *An American health dilemma.* Volume Two: *Race, medicine, and health care in the United States, 1900–2000.* New York: Routledge, 2002.

Callen, Michael and Richard Berkowitz, with Joseph Sonnabend and Richard Dworkin. *How to have sex in an epidemic.* New York: News from the Front, 1983. Reprinted in Berkowitz, Richard. *Stayin' Alive: The invention of safe sex, A personal history,* 187–223. Cambridge, MA: Westview Press, 2003.

Campbell, Catherine and Brian Williams. "Beyond the biomedical and behavioural: Towards an integrated approach to HIV prevention in the Southern African mining industry." *Social science and medicine* 48 (1999): 1625–1639.

Centers for Disease Control and Prevention (CDC). "*Pneumocystis* pneumonia—Los Angeles." *MMWR* 30 (June 5, 1981): 1–3. Accessed January 8, 2013. http://www.cdc.gov/mmwr/preview/mmwrhtml/june_5.htm.

———. "Antiretroviral postexposure prophylaxis after sexual, injection-drug use, or other nonoccupational exposure to HIV in the United States: Recommendations from the U.S. Department of Health and Human Services." *MMWR* 54.RR-2 (2005): 1–19.

———. "New CDC analysis reveals strong link between poverty and HIV infection." Press release, July 19, 2010. Accessed July 23, 2010. http://www.cdc.gov/nchhstp/newsroom/povertyandhivpressrelease.html.

———. "Characteristics associated with HIV infection among heterosexuals in urban areas with high AIDS prevalence—24 cities, United States, 2006–2007." *MMWR* 60 (2011): 1045–1049.

———. "Estimated HIV incidence in the United States, 2007– 2010." *HIV Surveillance Supplemental Report* 17 (2012). Accessed February 18, 2013. http://www.cdc.gov/hiv/topics/surveillance/resources/reports/ #supplemental.

———. "Prevalence of undiagnosed HIV infection among persons aged ≥13 years—National HIV surveillance system, United States, 2005–2008." *MMWR* 61, suppl (June 15, 2012): 57–64.

———. "HIV among African Americans." Fact Sheet. Last updated February 2013. Accessed March 23, 2013. http://www.cdc.gov/hiv/pdf/risk_HIV_AAA.pdf.

Chandra, Ranjit Kumar. "Nutrition and the immune system: An introduction." *American journal of clinical nutrition* 66 (1997): 460S–463S.

Chauncey, George. *Gay New York: Gender, urban culture, and the making of the gay male world, 1890–1940.* New York: Basic Books, 1994.

Chowkwanyun, Merlin. "The strange disappearance of history from racial health disparities research." *Du Bois review* 8 (2011): 253–270.

Clear, Todd R. *Imprisoning communities: How mass incarceration makes disadvantaged neighborhoods worse.* New York: Oxford University Press, 2007.

Cochrane, Michelle. *When AIDS began: San Francisco and the making of an epidemic.* New York: Routledge, 2004.

Cohen, Cathy J. "Punks, bulldaggers and welfare queens: The radical potential of queer politics?" *GLQ* 3 (1997): 437–466.

———. *The boundaries of blackness: AIDS and the breakdown of black politics.* Chicago: University of Chicago Press, 1999.

———. "Deviance as resistance: A new research agenda for the study of Black politics." *Du Bois review* 1 (2004): 27–45.

Cohen, Myron S. "HIV prevention: Rethinking the risk of transmission." *IAVA report* 8 (September-November 2004): 1–4. Accessed October 19, 2013, from http://www.iavireport.org/Back-Issues/Pages/IAVI-Report-08(3)-HIVPreventionRethinkingtheRiskofTransmission.aspx.

Collins, Patricia Hill. *Black sexual politics: African Americans, gender, and the new racism.* New York: Routledge, 2004.

Comfort, Megan. "Punishment beyond the legal offender." *Annual review of law and social science* 3 (2007): 271–296.

Connolly, Máire A. and David L. Heymann. "Deadly comrades: War and infectious diseases." *The Lancet* 360 (2002): s23–s24.

Crenshaw, Kimberlé Williams. "Demarginalizing the intersections of race and sex: A Black feminist critique of antidiscrimination doctrine, feminist theory and antiracist politics." *University of Chicago legal forum* 4 (1989): 139–167.

———. "Color-blind dreams and racial nightmares: Reconfiguring racism in the post-civil rights era." In *Birth of a nation'hood: Gaze, script, and spectacle in the O.J. Simpson case,* edited by Toni Morrison and Claudia Brodsky Lacour, 97–168. New York: Pantheon Books, 1997.

Crimp, Douglas. "AIDS: Cultural analysis/cultural activism." In *AIDS: Cultural analysis, cultural activism,* edited by Douglas Crimp, 3–16. Cambridge: The MIT Press, 1988.

———. "How to have promiscuity in an epidemic." In *AIDS: Cultural analysis, cultural activism,* edited by Douglas Crimp, 237–268. Cambridge: The MIT Press, 1988.

———. *Melancholia and moralism: Essays on AIDS and queer politics.* Cambridge, MA: The MIT Press, 2002.

———. "Randy Schilts's miserable failure." In *Melancholia and moralism: Essays on AIDS and queer politics,* 117–128. Cambridge, MA: The MIT Press, 2002.

Crimp, Douglas, ed. *AIDS: Cultural Analysis, Cultural Activism.* Cambridge: The MIT Press, 1988.

Cunningham-Rundles, Susanna. "Analytical methods for evaluation of immune response in nutrient intervention." *Nutrition reviews* 56, no. 1, pt. 2 (1998): S27–37.

Davis, Angela Y. *Women, race & class.* New York: Vintage Books, 1983.

———. *Are prisons obsolete?* New York: Seven Stories Press, 2003.

de Certeau, Michel. *The practice of everyday life.* Translated by Steven Rendall. Berkeley: University of California Press, 1984.

Denizet-Lewis, Benoit. "Double lives on the down low." *The New York Times Magazine,* August 3, 2003.

Denning, Paul and Elizabeth DiNenno. "Communities in Crisis: Is there a generalized HIV epidemic in impoverished urban areas of the United States?" Poster presentation, July 18–23, 2010. *AIDS 2010: XVIII International AIDS Conference.* Vienna, Austria.

Du Bois, William Edward Burghardt. "The health and physique of the Negro American." 1906. *American journal of public health* 93 (February 2003): 272–276.

Duggan, Lisa. *The twilight of equality? Neoliberalism, cultural politics, and the attack on democracy.* Boston: Beacon Press, 2003.

Duster, Troy. "Lessons from history: Why race and ethnicity have played a major role in biomedical research." *Journal of law, medicine and ethics* 34 (2006): 487–496.

Dyer, Richard. "The role of stereotypes." In *The matter of images: Essays on representations,* 11–18. New York: Routledge, 1993.

Engels, Frederick. *The condition of the working class in England.* 1845. London: Grenada Publishing, 1962.

Epprecht, Marc. *Heterosexual Africa? The history of an idea from the age of exploration to the age of AIDS.* Athens, OH: Ohio State University Press, 2008.

Epstein, Steven. *Inclusion: The politics of difference in medical research.* Chicago: University of Chicago Press, 2007.

Esposito, Roberto. *Bios: Biopolitics and philosophy.* Translated by Timothy Campbell. Minneapolis: University of Minnesota Press, 2008.

Estébanez, P., M. V. Zunzunegui, M. D. Aguilar, N. Russell, I. Cifuentes, and C. Hankins. "The role of prisons in the HIV epidemic among female injecting drug users." *AIDS care* 14 (2002): 95–104.

Fairchild, Amy L. and Ronald Bayer. "Uses and abuses of Tuskegee." *Science* 284 (1999): 919–921.

Fanon, Frantz. *Black Skin, White Masks.* Translated by Charles Lam Markmann. New York: Grove Weidenfeld, 1967.

Farmer, Paul. *Infections and inequalities: The modern plagues.* Paperback edition. Berkeley: University of California Press, 2001.

———. "Rethinking 'emerging infectious diseases.'" In *Infections and inequality: The modern plagues,* 37–58. Berkeley: University of California Press, 2001.

———. *AIDS and accusation: Haiti and the geography of blame.* Updated edition. Berkeley: University of California Press, 2006.

———. "Women, poverty, and AIDS." In *Women, poverty, and AIDS: Sex, drugs, and structural violence*, edited by Paul Farmer, Margaret Connors, and Janie Simmons, 3–38. Second edition. Monroe, ME: Common Courage Press, 2011.

Farmer, Paul and Jim Yong Kim. "Introduction to the first edition." In *Women, poverty, and AIDS: Sex, drugs, and structural violence*, edited by Paul Farmer, Margaret Connors, and Janie Simmons, xxxvii–xlv. Second edition. Monroe, ME: Common Courage Press, 2011.

Farmer, Paul, Margaret Connors, and Janie Simmons, eds. *Women, poverty, and AIDS: Sex, drugs, and structural violence*. Second edition. Monroe, ME: Common Courage Press, 2011.

Fassin, Didier. "Embodied history: Uniqueness and exemplarity of South African AIDS." *African journal of AIDS research* 1 (2002): 63–68.

———. "The embodiment of inequality." *EMBO reports* 4 (2003): S4–9.

———. *When bodies remember: Experience and politics of AIDS in South Africa*. Translated by Amy Jacobs and Gabrielle Varro. Berkeley: University of California Press, 2007.

Fausto-Sterling, Anne. "The problem with sex/gender and nature/nurture." In *Debating biology: Sociological reflections on health, medicine, and society*, edited by Simon J. Williams, Lynda Birke, and Gillian A. Bendelow, 123–132. New York: Routledge, 2003.

———. "Refashioning race: DNA and the politics of health care." *Differences: A journal of feminist cultural studies* 15 (2004): 1–37.

———. "The bare bones of sex: part 1—Sex and gender." *Signs: Journal of women in culture and society* 30 (2005): 1491–1527.

———. "Frameworks of Desire." *Daedalus* 136 (2007): 47–57.

Fee, Elizabeth and Daniel M. Fox, eds. *AIDS: The burdens of history*. Berkeley: University of California Press, 1988.

Fee, Elizabeth and Nancy Krieger. "Understanding AIDS: Historical interpretations and the limits of biomedical individualism." *American journal of public health* 83 (1993): 1477–1486.

Feldman, Eric A. and Ronald Bayer, eds. *Blood feuds: AIDS, blood, and the politics of medical disaster*. New York: Oxford University Press, 1999.

Ferguson, Roderick A. *Aberrations in Black: Toward a queer of color critique*. Minneapolis: University of Minnesota Press, 2004.

Fine, Paul E. M. "Herd immunity: History, theory, practice." *Epidemiologic reviews* 15 (1993): 265–302.

Foucault, Michel. *The history of sexuality, volume 1: An introduction*. Translated by Robert Hurley. New York: Vintage Books, 1990.

Foucault, Michel. "Governmentality." In *The Foucault Effect: Studies in governmentality*, edited by Graham Burchell, Colin Gordon, and Peter Miller, 87–104. Chicago: The University of Chicago Press, 1991.

———. "About the concept of the 'dangerous individual' in nineteenth-century legal psychiatry." In *Power*, edited by James D. Faubion, 176–200. New York: The New Press, 2000.

———. *"Society must be defended:" Lectures at the Collège de France, 1975–1976.* Translated by David Macey. New York: Picador, 2003.

Geary, Adam. "Culture as an object of ethical governance in AIDS prevention." *Cultural Studies* 21 (2007): 672–694.

———. "Inessential theory: Culture and AIDS risk governance." *Eä: Journal of medical humanities and social studies of science and technology* 2 (April 2011). www.ea-journal.com.

Geronimus, Arline T. "To mitigate, resist, or undo: Addressing structural influences on the health of urban populations." *American journal of public health* 90 (2000): 867–872.

Geronimus, Arline T., John Bound, and Timothy A. Waidmann. "Poverty, time and place: Variation in excess mortality across selected U.S. populations, 1980–1990." *Journal of epidemiology and community health* 53 (1999): 325–334.

Geronimus, Arline T. and J. Phillip Thompson. "To denigrate, ignore, or disrupt: Racial inequality in health and the impact of a policy-induced breakdown of African American communities." *Du Bois Review* 1 (2004): 247–279.

Gillespie, Stuart, ed. *AIDS, poverty, and hunger: Challenges and responses.* Highlights of the International Conference on HIV/AIDS and Food and Nutrition Security, Durban, South Africa, April 14–16, 2005. Washington, DC: International Food Policy Research Institute, 2006.

Gilmore, Ruth Wilson. *Golden Gulag: Prisons, surplus, crisis, and opposition in globalizing California.* Berkeley and Los Angeles: University of California Press, 2007.

Gisselquist, David. "Estimating HIV-1 transmission efficiency through unsafe medical injections," *International journal of STD & AIDS* 13 (2002): 152–159.

Gisselquist, David, Richard Rothenberg, John Potterat, and Ernest Drucker. "HIV infections in sub-Saharan Africa not explained by sexual or vertical transmission." *International journal of STD & AIDS* 13 (2002): 657–666.

Glick Schiller, Nina. "What's wrong with this picture? The hegemonic construction of culture in AIDS research in the United States." *Medical anthropology quarterly* 6 (1992): 237–254.

Glick Schiller, Nina, Stephen Crystal, and Denver Lewellen. "Risky business: An examination of the cultural construction of AIDS risk groups." *Social science and medicine* 38 (1994): 1337–1346.

Goldberg, David Theo. "Racism without racism." *PMLA* 123 (2008): 1712–1716.

Gordon, Colin. "Governmental rationality: An introduction." In *The Foucault Effect: Studies in governmentality*, edited by Graham Burchell, Colin Gordon, and Peter Miller, 1–51. Chicago: The University of Chicago Press, 1991.

Gould, Peter. *The slow plague: A geography of the AIDS pandemic*. Oxford: Blackwell Publisher, 1993.

———. *Becoming a geographer*. Syracuse, NY: Syracuse University Press, 1999.

Grmek, Mirko D. *History of AIDS: Emergence and origin of a modern pandemic*. Translated by Russell C. Maulitz and Jacalyn Duffin. Princeton: Princeton University Press, 1990.

Gupta, Kalpana and Per Johan Klasse. "How do viral and host factors modulate the sexual transmission of HIV? Can transmission be blocked?" *PLoS Med* 3 (2006): e79. doi: 10.1371/journal.pmed.0030079.

Hall, Stuart. "Race, articulation, and societies structured in dominance." In *Sociological theories: Race and colonialism*, edited by Colette Guillaumin, 305–345. Paris: UNESCO, 1980.

Hammonds, Evelynn M. "Seeing AIDS: Race, gender, and representation." In *The gender politics of HIV/AIDS in women: Perspectives on the pandemic in the United States*, edited by Nancy Goldstein and Jennifer L. Manlowe, 113–126. New York: New York University Press, 1997.

———. "Toward a genealogy of black female sexuality: The problematic of silence." In *Feminist genealogies, colonial legacies, democratic futures*, edited by M. Jacqui Alexander and Chandra Talpade Mohanty, 170–182. New York: Routledge, 1997.

Hartman, Saidiya. *Lose your mother: A journey along the Atlantic slave route*. New York: Farrar, Straus and Giroux, 2007.

Hayward, Mark D., Toni P. Miles, Eileen M. Crimmins, and Yu Yang. "The significance of socioeconomic status in explaining the racial gap in chronic health conditions." *American sociological review* 65 (2000): 910–930.

Herman, Arthur. *The Idea of Decline in Western History*. New York: The Free Press, 1997.

hooks, bell. *Ain't I a Woman: Black women and feminism*. Boston: South End Press, 1981.

Hooper, Edward. *The river: A journey to the source of HIV and AIDS*. New York: Little, Brown and Company, 1999.

Iguchi, Martin Y., James Bell, Rajeev N. Ramchand, and Terry Fain. "How criminal system racial disparities may translate into health disparities." *Journal of health care for the poor and underserved* 16, no. 4, suppl. B (2005): 48–56.

Iqbal, Shehzad M. and Rupert Kaul. "Mucosal innate immunity as a determinant of HIV susceptibility." *American journal of reproductive immunology* 59 (2008): 44–54.

James, Joy, ed. *Warfare in the American homeland: Policing and prison in a penal democracy.* Durham: Duke University Press, 2007.

Jargowsky, Paul A. *Poverty and place: Ghettos, barrios, and the American city.* New York: Russell Sage Foundation, 1997.

John, T. Jacob and Reuben Samuel. "Herd immunity and herd effect: New insights and definitions." *European journal of epidemiology* 16 (2000): 601–606.

Johnson, Rucker C. and Steven Raphael. "The effects of male incarceration dynamics on Acquired Immune Deficiency Syndrome infection rates among African American women and men." *Journal of law and economics* 52 (2009): 251–293.

Jones, James H. *Bad Blood: The Tuskegee Syphilis Experiment.* New York: The Free Press, 1981.

Kalipeni, Ezekiel, Susan Craddock, Joseph R. Oppong, and Jayati Ghosh, eds. *HIV & AIDS in Africa: Beyond epidemiology.* Malden, MA: Blackwell Publishing, 2004.

Katz, Alison. "AIDS, individual behaviour and the unexplained remaining variation." *African journal of AIDS research* 1 (2002): 125–142.

Kaul, R., C. Pettengell, P. M. Sheth, S. Sunderji, A. Biringer, K. MacDonald, S. Walmsley, and A. Rebbapragada. "The genital tract immune milieu: An important determinant of HIV susceptibility and secondary transmission." *Journal of reproductive immunology* 77 (2008): 32–40.

Keusch, Gerald T. "The history of nutrition: Malnutrition, infection and immunity." *Journal of nutrition* 133 (2003): 336S–340S.

King, Edward. *Safety in numbers: Safer sex and gay men.* Forward by Cindy Patton. New York: Routledge, 1993.

Kinsman, Gary. "Managing AIDS organizing: 'Consultation,' 'partnership,' and 'responsibility' as strategies of regulation." In *Organizing dissent: Contemporary social movements in theory and practice,* edited by W. K. Carroll, 213–239. Toronto: Garamond Press, 1992.

———. "'Responsibility' as a strategy of governance: Regulating people living with AIDS and lesbians and gay men in Ontario." *Economy and society* 25 (1996): 394–409.

Krieger, Nancy. "Epidemiology and the web of causation: Has anyone seen the spider?" *Social science and medicine* 39 (1994): 887–903.

———. "A glossary for social epidemiology." *Journal of epidemiology and community health* 55 (2001): 693–700.

———. "Theories for social epidemiology in the 21st century: An ecosocial perspective." *International journal of epidemiology* 30 (2001): 668–677.

———. "Does racism harm health? Did child abuse exist before 1962? On explicit questions, critical science, and current controversies: an ecosocial perspective." *American journal of public health* 93 (2003): 194–199.

———. "Stormy Weather: Race, gene expression, and the science of health disparities." *American journal of public health* 95 (2005): 2155–2160.

———. *Epidemiology and the people's health: Theory and context.* New York: Oxford, 2011.

Krieger, Nancy, Diane L. Rowley, Allen A. Herman, Byllye Avery, and Mona T. Phillips. "Racism, sexism, and social class: Implications for studies of health, disease, and well-being." *American journal of preventive medicine* 9 (1993): 82–122.

Krieger, Nancy and Stephen Sidney. "Racial discrimination and blood pressure: The Cardia study of young black and white adults." *American journal of public health* 86 (1996): 1370–1378.

Lane, Sandra D., Robert A. Rubinstein, Robert H. Keefe, Noah Webster, Donald A. Cibula, Alan Rosenthal, and Jesse Dowdell. "Structural violence and racial disparity in HIV transmission." *Journal of health care for the poor and underserved* 15 (2004): 319–335.

Lefree, Gary, Kriss A. Drass, and Patrick O'Day. "Race and crime in post-war America: Determinants of African American and white rates, 1957–1988." *Criminology* 30 (1992): 157–188.

Link, Bruce G. and Jo Phelan. "Social conditions as fundamental causes of disease." *Journal of health and social behavior* 35, extra issue (1995): 80–94.

London, Andrew S. and Nancy A. Myers. "Race, incarceration, and health: A life-course approach." *Research on aging* 28 (2006): 409–422.

Lorde, Audre. *Sister outsider: Essays and speeches.* Berkeley: Crossing Press, 1984.

———. "Apartheid U.S.A." In *I am your sister: Collected and unpublished writings of Audre Lorde,* edited by Rudolph P. Byrd, Johnnetta Betsch Cole, and Beverly Guy-Scheftall, 64–72. New York: Oxford University Press, 2009.

Lupton, Deborah. *The imperative of health: Public health and the regulated body.* Thousand Oaks, CA: Sage, 1995.

Lyons, Maryinez. "Mobile populations and HIV/AIDS in East Africa." In *HIV & AIDS in Africa: Beyond epidemiology*, edited by Ezekiel Kalipeni, Susan Craddock, Joseph R. Oppong, and Jayati Ghosh, 175–190. Malden, MA: Blackwell Publishing, 2004.

Magnus, Manya, Irene Kuo, Gregory Phillips II, Katharine Shelley, Anthony Rawls, Luz Montanez, James Peterson, Tiffany West-Ojo, Shannon Hader, and Alan E. Greenberg. "Elevated HIV prevalence despite lower rates of sexual risk behaviors among black men in the District of Columbia who have sex with men." *AIDS patient care and STDs* 24 (2010): 615–622.

Malvy, D. "Micronutrients and tropical viral infections: One aspect of pathogenic complexity in tropical medicine." *Médécine tropicale* 59, no. 4, part 2 (1999): 442–448.

Marable, Manning. "Structural racism and American democracy: Historical and theoretical perspectives." *Souls: A critical journal of Black politics, culture, and society* 3 (Winter 2001): 6–24.

Marmot, Michael G., Geoffrey Rose, Martin J. Shipley, and Peter J. Hamilton. "Employment grade and coronary heart disease in British civil servants." *Journal of epidemiology and community health* 32 (1978): 244–249.

Marshall, Stuart. "Picturing deviancy." In *Ecstatic antibodies: Resisting the AIDS mythology*, edited by Tessa Boffin and Sunil Gupta, 19–36. London: Rivers Oram Press, 1990.

Marshall, Wende Elizabeth. "AIDS, race and the limits of science." *Social science and medicine* 60 (2005): 2515–2525.

Maruschak, Laura M. and Allen J. Beck. "Medical problems of inmates." Bureau of Justice Statistics Special Report, NCJ 181644. U.S. Department of Justice, 2001.

Massey, Douglas S. "American apartheid: Segregation and the making of the underclass." *American journal of sociology* 96 (1990): 329–357.

Massey, Douglas S. and Nancy A. Denton. "Hypersegregation in U.S. metropolitan areas: Black and hispanic segregation along five dimensions." *Demography* 26 (1989): 373–391.

———. *American apartheid: Segregation and the making of the underclass.* Cambridge, MA: Harvard University Press, 1993.

Massey, Douglas and Zoltan L. Hajnal. "The changing geographic structure of black-white segregation in the United States." *Social science quarterly* 76 (1995): 527–542.

Massoglia, Michael. "Incarceration, health, and racial disparities in health." *Law and society review* 42 (2008): 275–306.

Massoglia, Michael and Jason Schnittker. "No real release." *Contexts* 8 (2009): 38–42. Accessed September 11, 2011. www.contexts.org.

Mauer, Marc and Meda Chesney-Lind, eds. *Invisible punishment: The collateral consequences of mass imprisonment.* New York: The New Press, 2002.

Mauer, Marc and Ryan S. King. "Uneven justice: State rates of incarceration by race and ethnicity." *The Sentencing Project.* Last updated 2007. Accessed December 27, 2011. http://www.sentencingproject .org/doc/publications/rd_stateratesofincbyraceandethnicity.pdf.

Mauer, Marc and The Sentencing Project. *Race to incarcerate.* Second edition. New York: The New Press, 2006.

McBride, David. *From TB to AIDS: Epidemics among urban blacks since 1900.* Albany: State University of New York Press, 1991.

McMurray, David. "Impact of nutritional deficiencies on resistance to experimental pulmonary tuberculosis." *Nutrition reviews* 56, no.1, pt. 2 (1998): S147–152.

Millet, Gregorio A. and John L. Peterson. "The known hidden epidemic: HIV/AIDS among black men who have sex with men in the United States." *American journal of preventive medicine* 32 (2007): S31–S33

Millet, Gregorio A., John L. Peterson, Richard J. Wolitski, and Ron Stall. "Greater risk for HIV infection of black men who have sex with men: A critical literature review." *American journal of public health* 96 (2006): 1007–1019.

Millet, Gregorio A., Stephen A. Flores, John L. Peterson, and Roger Bakeman. "Explaining disparities in HIV infection among black and white men who have sex with men: A meta-analysis of HIV risk behaviors." *AIDS* 21 (2007): 2083–2091.

Mindry, Deborah. "Neoliberalism, activism, and HIV/AIDS in postapartheid South Africa." *Social Text* no. 94 (2008): 75–93

Mohanty, Chandra Talpade. "Under western eyes: Feminist scholarship and colonial discourses." In *Third world women and the politics of feminism*, edited by Chandra Talpade Mohanty, Ann Russo, and Lourdes Torres, 51–80. Bloomington: Indiana University Press, 1991.

Moore, Richard D., Jeanne C. Keruly, and John G. Bartlett. "Improvement in the health of HIV-infected persons in care: Reducing disparities." *Clinical infectious diseases* 55 (2012): 1242–1251.

Morrison, Toni. *Playing in the dark: Whiteness and the literary imagination.* New York: Vintage Books, 1993.

Morrow, Gavin, Laurence Vachot, Panagiotis Vagenas, and Melissa Robbiani. "Current concepts of HIV transmission." *Current HIV/ AIDS reports* 4 (2007): 29–35.

Morse, Stephen S. "Factors in the emergence of infectious diseases." *Emerging infectious diseases* 1 (1995): 7–15.

Mukherjee, Joia. "Preface to the second edition." In *Women, poverty, and AIDS: Sex, drugs, and structural violence*, edited by Paul Farmer, Margaret Connors, and Janie Simmons, ix–xxii. Second edition. Monroe, ME: Common Courage Press, 2011.

National Minority Quality Forum. *U.S. HIV/AIDS index*. Washington, DC: National Minority Quality Forum, 2011. Accessed February 26, 2013. http://www.maphiv.org.

National Research Council. *The social impact of AIDS in the United States*. Washington, DC: The National Academy of Sciences, 1993.

Navarro, Vicente. "U.S. Marxist scholarship in the analysis of health and medicine." *International journal of health services* 15 (1985): 525–545.

Nelson, Alondra. *Body and soul: The Black Panther Party and the fight against medical discrimination*. Minneapolis: University of Minnesota Press, 2011.

Newman, Lori M. and Stuart M. Berman. "Epidemiology of STD disparities in African American communities." *Sexually transmitted diseases* 35, December suppl. (2008): S4–S12.

O'Manique, Colleen. *Neoliberalism and AIDS epidemic in Sub-Saharan Africa: Globalization's pandemic*. New York: Palgrave Macmillan, 2004.

Odets, Walt. "On the need for a gay reconstruction of public health." In *A Queer World: The center for lesbian and gay studies reader*, edited by Martin Duberman, 668–676. New York: New York University Press, 1997.

Office of National AIDS Policy. *National HIV/AIDS strategy for the United States*. Washington, DC: Office of National AIDS Policy, 2010. Accessed May 13, 2013. http://www.whitehouse.gov/administration/eop/onap/nhas.

Oguntibeju, O. O., W. M. J. van den Heever, and F. E. Van Schalkwyk. "The interrelationship between nutrition and the immune system in HIV infection: A review." *Pakistan journal of biological sciences* 10 (2007): 4327–4338.

Omi, Michael and Howard Winant. *Racial formation in the United States: From the 1960s to the 1990s*. Second edition. New York: Routledge, 1994.

Oppenheimer, Gerald M. "In the eye of the storm: The epidemiological construction of AIDS." In *AIDS: The burdens of history*, edited by Elizabeth Fee and Daniel M. Fox, 267–300. Berkeley: University of California Press, 1988.

Patterson, Orlando. *Slavery and social death: A comparative study.* Cambridge, MA: Harvard University Press, 1985.

Patton, Cindy. "Heterosexual AIDS panic: A queer paradigm." *Gay community news* (Boston), February 9, 1985, 3, 6.

———. *Sex and germs: The politics of AIDS.* Boston: South End Press, 1985.

———. *Inventing AIDS.* New York: Routledge, 1990.

———. "From nation to family: Containing African AIDS." In *The lesbian and gay studies reader,* edited by Henry Abelove, Michèle Aina Barale, and David Halperin, 127–138. New York: Routledge, 1993.

———. *Last served? Gendering the HIV pandemic.* Bristol, PA: Taylor & Francis Inc., 1994.

———. *Fatal advice: How safe-sex education went wrong.* Durham: Duke University Press, 1996.

———. *Globalizing AIDS.* Minneapolis: University of Minnesota Press, 2002.

Pettit, Becky and Bruce Western. "Mass imprisonment and the life course: Race and class inequality in U.S. incarceration." *American sociological review* 69 (2004): 151–169.

Phillips, Layli. "Deconstructing 'down low' discourse: The politics of sexuality, gender, race, AIDS, and anxiety." *Journal of African American studies* 9 (2005): 3–15.

Piot, Peter, Francis A. Plummer, Fred S. Mhalu, Jean-Louis Lamboray, James Chin, and Jonathan M. Mann. "AIDS: An international perspective." *Science* 239 (1988): 573–579. Accessed July 25, 2013. www .sciencemag.org.

Piot, Peter, Marie Laga, Robert Ryder, Jos Perriens, Marleen Temmerman, William Heyward, and James W. Curran. "The global epidemiology of HIV infection: Continuity, heterogeneity, and change." *Journal of acquired immune deficiency syndrome* 3 (1990): 403–412.

Poku, Nana K. "Africa's AIDS crisis in context: 'How the poor are dying.'" *Third world quarterly* 22 (2001): 191–204.

Porter, Dorothy. "How did social medicine evolve, and where is it heading?" *PLoS Med* 3 (2006): e399. Accessed December 3, 2010. doi: 10.1371/journal.pmEdited by0030399.

Poundstone, K.E., S.A. Strathdee, and D.D. Celentano. "The social epidemiology of human immunodeficiency virus/acquired immunodeficiency syndrome." *Epidemiologic reviews* 26 (2004): 22–35.

Quinn, Thomas C., Maria J. Wawer, Nelson Sewankambo, David Serwadda, Chuanjun Li, Fred Wabwire-Mangen, Mary O. Meehan, Thomas Lutalo, and Ronald H. Gray. "Viral load and heterosexual transmission of human immunodeficiency virus type 1." *New England journal of medicine* 342 (2000): 921–929.

Rhodes, Tim. "The 'risk environment:' A framework for understanding and reducing drug-related harm." *International journal of drug policy* 13 (2002): 85–94.

Rhodes, Tim and Milena Simic. "Transition and the HIV risk environment." *BMJ* 331 (2005): 220–223.

Rise of the Planet of the Apes. Directed by Rupert Wyatt. Film. Twentieth Century Fox Film Corporation, 2011.

Roberts, Dorothy. *Killing the Black body: Race, reproduction, and the meaning of liberty.* Vintage Books edition. New York: Vintage Books, 1999.

———. *Shattered bonds: The color of child welfare.* New York: Basic Civitas Books, 2003.

———. *Fatal invention: How science, politics, and big business re-create race in the twenty-first century.* New York: The New Press, 2011.

Rosen, George. *A history of public health.* 1958. Baltimore, MD: The Johns Hopkins University Press, 1993.

Rowden, Rick. *The deadly ideas of neoliberalism.* New York: Zed Books, 2009.

Rushton, J. Phillipe. *Race, evolution and behavior: A life history perspective.* New Brunswick, NJ: Transaction, 1997.

Sampson, Robert J. and Janet R. Lauritson. "Racial and ethnic disparities in crime and criminal justice in the United States." In *Ethnicity, crime, and immigration: Comparative and cross-national perspectives*, edited by Michael Tonry, 311–374. Chicago: University of Chicago Press, 1997.

Sander, David and Abdulrahman Sambo. "AIDS in Africa: The implications of economic recession and structural adjustment." *Health policy and planning* 6 (1991): 157–165.

Sawers, Larry and Eileen Stillwaggon. "Concurrent sexual partnerships do not explain the HIV epidemics in Africa: A systematic review of the evidence." *Journal of the International AIDS Society* 13 (2010): e34, doi: 10.1186/1758-2652-13-34.

Scheper-Hughes, Nancy. "AIDS and the social body." *Social science and medicine* 39 (1994): 991–1003.

Schneider, William H. and Earnest Drucker. "Blood transfusions in the early years of AIDS in Sub-Saharan Africa." *American journal of public health* 96 (2006): 984–994.

Schnittker, Jason, Michael Massoglia, and Christopher Uggen. "Incarceration and the health of the African American community." *Du Bois Review* 8 (2011): 1–9.

Schoepf, Brooke Grundfest. "Gender, development, and AIDS: A political economy and culture framework." *Women and international development annual* 3 (1993): 53–85.

———. "AIDS, history, and struggles over meaning." In *HIV & AIDS in Africa: Beyond epidemiology*, edited by Ezekiel Kalipeni, Susan Craddock, Joseph R. Oppong, and Jayati Ghosh, 15–28. Malden, MA: Blackwell Publishing, 2004.

———. "AIDS in Africa: Structure, agency, and risk." In *HIV & AIDS in Africa: Beyond epidemiology*, edited by Ezekiel Kalipeni, Susan Craddock, Joseph R. Oppong, and Jayati Ghosh, 121–132. Malden, MA: Blackwell Publishing, 2004.

Scrimshaw, Nevin S. and John Paul SanGiovanni. "Synergism of nutrition, infection, and immunity: An overview." *American journal of clinical nutrition* 66 (1997): 464S–477S.

Sedgwick, Eve Kosofsky. "Epidemics of the will." In *Tendencies*, 130–142. Durham: Duke University Press, 1993.

Semba, Richard D. "The role of vitamin A and related retinoids in immune function." *Nutrition reviews* 56, no. 1, pt. 2 (1998): S38–48.

Sentencing Project, The. "The Sentencing Project news – Incarceration." *The Sentencing Project.* n.d. Accessed December 27, 2011. http://www.sentencingproject.org/template/page.cfm?id=107.

Sexton, Jared. *Amalgamation schemes: Antiblackness and the critique of multiracialism.* Minneapolis: University of Minnesota Press, 2008.

———. "People-of-color-blindness: Notes on the afterlife of slavery." *Social Text* 28 (2010): 31–56.

Sexton, Jared and Elizabeth Lee. "Figuring the prison: Prerequisites of torture at Abu Ghraib." *Antipode* 38 (2006): 1005–1022.

Shabazz, Rashad. "Mapping black bodies for disease: Prisons, migration, and the politics of HIV/AIDS." In *Beyond walls and cages: Prisons, borders, and global crisis*, edited by Jenna M. Loyd, Matt Mitchelson, and Andrew Burridge, 287–300. Athens, GA: University of Georgia Press, 2012.

Shavers, Vickie L. and Brenda S. Shavers. "Racism and health inequality among Americans." *Journal of the national medical association* 98 (2006): 386–396.

Shilts, Randy. *And the band played on: Politics, people, and the AIDS epidemic.* New York: Penguin Books, 1988.

Singer, Merrill. "AIDS and the health crisis of the U.S. urban poor: the perspective of critical medical anthropology." *Social science and medicine* 39 (1994): 931–948.

Singer, Merrill, ed. *The political economy of AIDS.* Amityville, NY: Baywood Publishing Company, Inc., 1998.

Singer, Merrill, Candida Flores, Lani Davison, Georgine Burke, Zaida Castillo, Kelley Scanlon, and Migdalia Rivera. "SIDA: The economic, social, and cultural context of AIDS among Latinos." *Medical anthropology quarterly* 4 (1990): 72–114.

Singer, Merrill and Scott Clair. "Syndemics and public health: Reconceptualizing disease in bio-social context." *Medical anthropology quarterly* 17 (2003): 423–441.

Sitze, Adam. "Denialism." *The South Atlantic quarterly* 103 (2004): 769–811.

Smallman-Raynor, Matthew R., and Andrew D. Cliff. "Civil war and the spread of AIDS in Central Africa." *Epidemiology and infection* 107 (1991): 69–80.

———. *War epidemics: An historical geography of infectious diseases in military conflict and civil strife, 1850–2000.* Oxford: Oxford University Press, 2004.

Smith, Neil. "The satanic geographies of globalization: Uneven development in the 1990s." *Public culture* 10 (1997): 169–189.

Stark, Evan. "The epidemic as a social event." *International journal of health services* 7 (1977): 681–705.

———. "Doctors in spite of themselves: The limits of radical health criticism." *International journal of health services* 12 (1982): 419–457.

Starr, Paul. *The social transformation of American medicine.* New York: Basic Books, 1982.

Steinberg, Stephen. *Turning back: The retreat from racial justice in American thought and policy.* Boston: Beacon Press, 1995.

Stillwaggon, Eileen. "HIV transmission in Latin America: Comparison with Africa and policy implications." *South African journal of economics* 68 (2000): 985–1011.

———. *AIDS and the ecology of poverty.* New York: Oxford University Press, 2006.

———. "The ecology of poverty: Nutrition, parasites, and vulnerability to HIV/AIDS." In *AIDS, poverty, and hunger: Challenges and responses.* Highlights of the International Conference on HIV/AIDS and Food and Nutrition Security, Durban, South Africa, April 14–16, 2005, edited by Stuart Gillespie, 167–180. Washington, DC: International Food Policy Research Institute, 2006.

———. "Complexity, cofactors, and the failure of AIDS policy in Africa." *Journal of the International AIDS Society* 12 (2009): e12, doi: 10.1186/1758-2652-12-12.

Taylor, Rex and Annelie Rieger. "Rudolf Virchow on the typhus epidemic in Upper Silesia: An introduction and translation." *Sociology of health and illness* 6 (1984): 201–218.

Tesh, Sylvia Noble, *Hidden arguments: Political ideology and disease prevention policy.* New Brunswick, NJ: Rutgers University Press, 1994.

Thomas, Stephen B. and Sandra C. Quinn. "The Tuskegee Syphilis Study, 1932 to 1972: Implications for HIV education and AIDS risk education programs in Black communities." *American journal of public health* 81 (1991): 1498–1505.

Treichler, Paula A. "AIDS, Africa, and cultural theory." In *How to have theory in an epidemic: Cultural chronicles of AIDS*, 205–234. Durham: Duke University Press, 1999.

———. *How to have theory in an epidemic: Cultural chronicles of AIDS.* Durham: Duke University Press, 1999.

———. "The burdens of history: Gender and representation in AIDS discourse, 1981–1988." In *How to have theory in an epidemic: Cultural chronicles of AIDS*, 42–98. Durham: Duke University Press, 1999.

UNAIDS. *Global Report: UNAIDS report on the global AIDS epidemic, 2012.* Geneva, Switzerland: Joint United Nations Programme on HIV /AIDS, 2012. Accessed November 26, 2012. http://www.unaids.org /en/media/unaids/contentassets/documents/epidemiology/2012 /gr2012/20121120_UNAIDS_Global_Report_2012_en.pdf.

United States Census Bureau. *Population estimates.* Published July 1, 2010. Accessed March 3, 2013. http://www.census.gov/popest/data /intercensal/index.html.

———. *Income, poverty, and health insurance coverage in the United States: 2011.* Current Population Reports, P60–243. Washington, DC: U.S. Government Printing Office, 2012. Accessed May 20, 2013. http:// www.census.gov/prod/2012pubs/p60–243.pdf.

Unnatural causes: Is inequality making us sick? Series created and produced by Larry Adelman and Llewellyn M. Smith. San Francisco: California Newsreel, 2008.

Wacquant, Loïc. "Deadly symbiosis: When ghetto and prison meet and mesh." *Punishment & society* 3 (2001): 95–134.

———. "From slavery to mass incarceration: Rethinking the 'race question' in the US." *New left review* 13 (2002): 41–60.

———. "Gutting the ghetto: Political censorship and conceptual retrenchment in the American debate on urban destitution." In *Globalization and the new city: Migrants, minorities and urban transformation in comparative perspective*, edited by Malcome Cross and Robert Moore, 32–49. New York: Palgrave, 2002.

Wacquant, Loïc, Volker Eick, and Karen J. Winkler. "The wedding of workfare and prisonfare revisited." *Social justice* 38 (2011): 1–16.

Wakefield, Sara and Christopher Uggen. "Incarceration and stratification." *Annual review of sociology* 36 (2010): 387–406.

Wald, Priscilla. *Contagious: Cultures, carriers, and the outbreak narrative.* Durham: Duke University Press, 2008.

Wallace, Deborah and Roderick Wallace. *A plague on your houses: How New York was burned down and national public health crumbled.* New York: Verso, 1998.

Wallace, Roderick. "A synergism of plagues: "Planned shrinkage," contagious housing destruction, and AIDS in the Bronx." *Environmental research* 47 (1988): 1–33.

———. "Plague and power relations." *Geografiska annaler, series B: human geography* 89 (2007): 319–339.

Wallace, Roderick and Deborah Wallace. "U.S. apartheid and the spread of AIDS to the suburbs: A multi-city analysis of the political economy of spatial epidemic threshold." *Social science and medicine* 41 (1995): 333–345.

Wallace, Roderick, Deborah Wallace, J. E. Ullmann, and H. Andrews. "Deindustrialization, inner-city decay, and the hierarchical diffusion of AIDS in the USA: How neoliberal and cold war policies magnified the ecological niche for emerging infections and created a national security crisis." *Environment and planning* A31 (1999): 113–139.

Wallace, Roderick, and Robert Fullilove. "Why simple regression models work so well describing 'risk behaviors' in the USA." *Environment and planning* A31 (1999): 719–734.

Wallace, Roderick, Yi-Shan Huang, Peter Gould, and Deborah Wallace. "The hierarchical diffusion of AIDS and violent crime among U.S. metropolitan regions: Inner-city decay, stochastic resonance and reversal of the mortality transition." *Social science and medicine* 44 (1997): 935–947.

Ward, Martha C. "A different disease: HIV/AIDS and health care for women in poverty." *Culture, medicine and psychiatry* 17 (1993): 413–430.

Watney, Simon. "AIDS, 'moral panic' theory, and homophobia." In *Practices of freedom: Selected writings on HIV/AIDS*, 3–14. Durham: Duke University Press, 1994.

———. "Missionary positions: AIDS, 'Africa,' and race." In *Practices of freedom: Selected writings on HIV/AIDS*, 103–120. Durham: Duke University Press, 1994.

———. "Politics, people and the AIDS epidemic: *And the Band Played On*." In *Practices of freedom: Selected writings on HIV/AIDS*, 98–100. Durham: Duke University Press, 1994.

Wei, Chongyi, H. Fisher Raymond, Frank Y. Wong, Anthony J. Silvestre, Mark S. Friedman, Patricia Documét, Willi McFarland, and Ron Stall. "Lower HIV prevalence among Asian/Pacific Islander men who have sex with men: A critical review for possible reasons." *AIDS and behavior* 15 (2011): 535–649.

Weiss, Robin A. and Anthony J. McMichael. "Social and environmental risk factors in the emergence of infectious diseases." *Nature medicine* 10 (2004): S70–76.

Wildeman, Christopher. "Imprisonment and (inequality in) population health." University of Kentucky Center for Poverty Research Discussion Paper Series, DP2010–12. 2010. Accessed September 11, 2011. http://www.ukcpr.org/Publications/DP2010–12.pdf.

———. "(Mass) imprisonment and (inequities in) health." *American journal of epidemiology* 173 (2011): 488–491.

Wilderson III, Frank B. "Gramsci's black Marx: Whither the slave in civil society?" *Social identities* 9 (2003): 225–240.

———. *Red, white & black: Cinema and the structure of U.S. antagonisms.* Durham: Duke University Press, 2010.

Williams, David R. and Pamela Braboy Jackson. "Social sources of racial disparities in health." *Health affairs* 24 (2005): 325–334.

Williams, Simon J., Lynda Birke, and Gillian A. Bendelow, eds. *Debating biology: Sociological reflections on health, medicine, and society.* New York: Routledge, 2003.

Wilson, David. *Cities and race: America's new black ghetto.* New York: Routledge, 2007.

Wilton, James. "From exposure to infection: The biology of HIV transmission." *The Body: The complete HIV/AIDS resource (TheBody.com).* Last updated fall 2011. Accessed May 12, 2013. http://www.the body.com/content/68661/from-exposure-to-infection-the-biology -of-hiv-tran.html.

Woodward, Bill. "Protein, calories, and immune defense." *Nutrition reviews* 56, no. 1, pt. 2 (1998): S84–92.

Young, Iris Marion. "Five faces of oppression." In *Justice and the politics of difference,* 39–65. Princeton: Princeton University Press, 1990.

Zero patience. Directed by John Greyson. Film. Toronto: Cineplex Odeon Corporation, 1993.

Žižek, Slavoj. *Violence.* New York: Picador, 2008.

Index

Printed in the United States of America